NOAH ST. JOHN
#1 BESTSELLING AUTHOR OF

THE BOOK OF AFFORMATIONS®

CREATOR OF THE **POWER HABITS® SYSTEM** AND
FOUNDER OF **FREEDOM LIFESTYLE EXPERIENCE**

PRAISE FOR NOAH ST. JOHN

"Noah St. John's system represents one of the most significant break-throughs in the study of success in decades. If you want to eliminate the fear of success and live the life you've imagined, you owe it to yourself to get Noah's programs!"

— Jack Canfield, *Chicken Soup for the Soul*

"Noah St. John's work is about discovering within ourselves what we should have known all along—we are truly powerful beings with unlimited potential."

— Stephen Covey, *The 7 Habits of Highly Effective People*

"Noah St. John speaks the language we all want to understand: how to make the most of your life and career."

— Harvey Mackay, *Swim with the Sharks Without Being Eaten Alive*

"You'll never get your foot off the brake and find the success you dream of until you take Noah's advice to heart!"

— T. Harv Eker, *Secrets of the Millionaire Mind*

"Noah is a brilliant guy who brings tremendous insight into this problem of embracing success he quite accurately observes in people."

— Neale Donald Walsch, *Conversations with God*

"Noah has created something magical. I've been studying personal growth for more than 25 years and his insights take it to the next level!"

— Jenny McCarthy, Host of *The Jenny McCarthy Show*

"Using humor and down-to-earth language, Noah gives you a step-by-step method to live the life you want and deserve."

— John Gray, PhD, *Men Are from Mars, Women Are from Venus*

"If you are looking for a spark to light your inner flame, Noah's methods will IGNITE your passion within."

— John Lee Dumas, Host of *Entrepreneur on Fire*

"Noah St. John's work is awesome and sooooo very needed in this world right now!"

— Marie Forleo, Host of *MarieTV*

"Noah's methods can literally transform your life—and help you create the masterpiece you truly want and are capable of achieving."

— John Assaraf, *The Answer*

"Noah comes from his heart and shows you how to awaken to your own inner power—with the magic of a question."

— Dr. Joe Vitale, *The Attractor Factor*

"I went from $60,000 in debt to a six-figure income in six months because of Noah's trainings."

— Susan Sherayko, Television Producer

"I'd spent over $30,000 on self-improvement products with few results. By following Noah's program, my sales tripled in one month, and by the end of the year, my sales increased 560% and I was named New Agent of the Year."

— Brandon Handy, Allegis Financial Partners

"Noah's training was instrumental in helping me bounce back and into major profits. His insights on removing head trash are unlike anything I have ever seen!"

— Ray Higdon, Network Marketing Expert

"I went from $5,000 to $75,000 in monthly sales as a result of Noah's coaching. Best of all, I'm working FEWER hours than before, even with this increase in income. Thank you Noah for taking the lid off my thinking and letting me know I could have the BEST!"

— Sheila Valles, Entrepreneur

"Noah St. John helped me gain the mental edge I was looking for. His methods helped me perform at my highest level without strain, and I saw better results immediately using his system."

— Andre Branch, Miami Dolphins

"Our team has done amazing things because of Noah St. John's work. We had some people who were just blocked about life, and it has helped a ton. Personally I've lost 100 lbs, did a sprint triathlon, 5K and have now registered for a half marathon. I feel like I can take on the world! Getting rid of the head trash has been a huge part of my transformation. I learn something new every time I read or listen to Noah's work."

— Rob Hefley, Entrepreneur

"Before being mentored by Noah, I was holding myself back out of fear. Since working with Noah, I've built a multi-million dollar company in less than two years. I highly recommend Noah's coaching and mentoring, because I guarantee it will change your life like it changed mine."

— Tim Taylor, Real Estate Professional

"Great leaders know how to lead by example. They also know how to create trust. Noah St. John gives you a simple, proven way to become a true leader, both in your family as well as your professional life."

— Stephen M. R. Covey, *The Speed of Trust*

"Noah's work will help you understand what is important in your life and give you a clear path on believing in and achieving your goals. The sooner you start following Noah's program, the sooner your true happiness will begin."

— MaryEllen Tribby, Reinventing the Entrepreneur

"Before working with Noah, I was working like a slave 80 hours a week as an employee. After working with Noah, I now own my own business that brings in six figures per month. Plus, I found the love of my life using Noah's methods. Thank you Noah for believing in me when no one else did!"

— George Rivera, Entrepreneur

"To say that Noah St. John changed our lives is the understatement of the century. Before hiring Noah as my business coach, I had a brochure website that wasn't bringing in any money. Today I have my own online store, lead my own live events and have just written my first book. Thank you Noah for seeing greatness in me that I didn't know I had!"

— Dr. Stacey Cooper, Chiropractor

"Before I heard Noah speak, I had been a failure at everything I touched. After using his methods, I built the largest infill development company in Nashville with over $40 million in sales. Thank you Noah, keep doing what you're doing because a lot of people need you!"

— Britnie Turner Keane, CEO of Aerial Development Group

"Noah St. John is a heart-centered presenter and always makes me look like a hero to my audience members."

— Robert Jones, Founder of Network Together

"I highly recommend Noah St. John as a keynote speaker, because he's not only different from other speakers, he also really cares about his clients and resonates on a deep emotional level with his audience. He's dynamic, impactful, inspiring, motivating, and professional—in short, the PERFECT speaker!"

— Lauren Ashley Kay, Meeting Planner

"Noah's methods helped me get through a particularly challenging time in my life. If you're thinking about hiring Noah, I HIGHLY recommend it—because his strategies have the power to change lives!"

— Mari Smith, Premier Facebook Marketing Expert
& Social Media Thought Leader

ALSO AVAILABLE FROM NOAH ST. JOHN

POWER HABITS®

THE NEW SCIENCE FOR
MAKING SUCCESS AUTOMATIC®

NOAH ST. JOHN

Published and distributed by:
SOUND WISDOM
P.O. Box 310
Shippensburg, PA 17257-0310
717-530-2122

info@soundwisdom.com

www.soundwisdom.com

ISBN 13: 978-1-64095-096-2

ISBN 13 eBook: 978-1-64095-097-9

For Worldwide Distribution, Printed in the U.S.A.

Library of Congress Cataloging-in-Publication Data

Names: St. John, Noah, 1967- author.

Title: Power habits : the new science for making success automatic / Noah St. John.

Description: Shippensburg, PA : Sound Wisdom, [2019] | Includes bibliographical references and index. | Summary: "This is a book about creating the foundation for inner success that leads to and helps you maintain external success"—Provided by publisher.

Identifiers: LCCN 2019020985 (print) | LCCN 2019980653 (ebook) | ISBN 9781640950962 | ISBN 9781640950979 (ebook)

Subjects: LCSH: Success—Psychological aspects. | Happiness.

Classification: LCC BF637.S8 S684 2019 (print) | LCC BF637.S8 (ebook) | DDC 158--dc23

LC record available at https://lccn.loc.gov/2019020985

LC ebook record available at https://lccn.loc.gov/2019980653

1 2 3 4 5 6 7 8 / 23 22 21 20 19

This book is dedicated to #Afformers and #AfformationWarriors:

Those brave souls who ask better questions
to make this a better world
for all of God's creatures.

And to my beautiful wife Babette
for being the best example of a Loving Mirror
I've ever met.

CONTENTS

8

HOW THIS BOOK WAS WRITTEN—AND WHY

"The habit of reading is the only enjoyment in which there is no alloy; it lasts when all other pleasures fade."
— Anthony Trollope

Have you ever tried zip lining? If you haven't, have you ever wanted to try it?

In case you've never tried it, zip lining is an adventure sport where you strap yourself into a harness and go zooming through the air, suspended on a steel cable. After that description, maybe you're thinking, "I would NEVER try zip lining!"

Well, the truth is that I'm a total nerd, while my wife is a total adventure junkie (so of course we match perfectly). Before our wedding, we were planning our honeymoon—I was paying cash for our Caribbean cruise—when my bride-to-be says to me, "I know, let's go zip lining!"

And I'm thinking, *How can I get out of this?*

But of course I didn't want to look like a wimp to my bride-to-be, so I (with a great deal of hesitation) agreed.

On our honeymoon, I find myself on the island of St. Kitts, a stunningly beautiful gem in the middle of the Caribbean. However, because all I can think about is our upcoming zip lining adventure, I'm a nervous wreck.

We arrive at the zip lining location where three large, muscular men serve as our guides. They take us through a training process and give us harnesses and other gear. They also show us pictures of grandmothers and little kids who have done this—either as a way to calm us down or guilt us into not wimping out.

They then put our little zip lining group into a truck and drive us up a windy dirt road on the side of a mountain in the middle of a Caribbean rainforest. My heart is pounding a mile a minute. We go up, up, and up for what seems like forever...

We then pile out of the truck and climb up a set of wooden stairs to a small platform high up on the mountaintop.

> **I REALIZE THAT I HAVE THREE OPTIONS THAT WILL DEFINE THE REST OF MY LIFE.**

One of the large men straps on his gear, hooks onto the zip line, turns to us, and says, "See you on the other side!" and suddenly...

Zzzzzzzzzzzzzzzzzip! Off he goes off into infinity.

Gulp, says I.

Then one of the other large guides turns to me and says, "Okay, you're next."

Me??, I'm thinking. *Why do I have to go next?*

However, I still don't want to look like a coward in front of my new bride (even though I'm completely terrified), so I walk over to the edge of the platform and look down into infinity.

And my brain says to me: *We are definitely going to die.*

I realize that in the next few seconds, I have three options that will define the rest of my life.

OPTION 1: GO BACK, BECAUSE I'M TOO SCARED TO MOVE FORWARD.

My first thought is to go back to where we came from, back to the safety of the truck, and back to my old life—because I don't want to die.

Then I realize that going back is not really an option, because the truck has already left. Which means I would have to walk at least two miles down a windy dirt road on the side of a mountain in the middle of a Caribbean rainforest. Which means I could get eaten by crocagators or whatever else is lurking in the jungle. So I realize that the option to "go back" doesn't actually exist.

OPTION 2: STAY RIGHT WHERE I AM.

My second thought is that I could stay right where I am, don't move and don't go forward—because, as previously noted, I don't want to die.

Then I realize that staying where I am is not an option either, because how will I get down from the top of this mountain? It's not like they're going to just leave me standing there like an idiot (even though that's what I'd look like if I chose this option). And how will I face my new bride after wimping out like that?

So I realize that "staying where I am" is not really an option either. Finally, I review my other, and only realistic, option...

OPTION 3: FACE MY FEARS AND TAKE A STEP FORWARD.

As I'm standing there at the top of a mountain in the Caribbean rainforest pondering my certain death, suddenly a thought occurs to me:

Hey, wait a minute...that guide who went before me...he's bigger than me... which means he weighs more than I do...and he didn't die. So maybe I won't die, either!

Then I remember the training process with those pictures little kids and grandmothers doing zip lining, and I'm like: *Are you really going to wimp out when people just like you weren't afraid to do this, and THEY didn't die?*

So in that moment, I take a deep breath, and with my mind still screaming, *We're going to die!*, take that one step into infinity, and...

Wheeeeeeeeeeeeeeeee!

It's so fun, so exhilarating, I can't wait to do it again!

Here's a picture of me and my wife after I took ACTION in the face of fear:

Noah & Babette after Noah took ACTION in the face of fear!

18

In fact, I had such a great time that now, I lead zip lining adventures with my **Platinum and VIP Coaching clients** where I help impact-driven entrepreneurs supercharge their business to $100K a year (and beyond) without "tech overwhelm."

Here's a picture of one of our VIP Inner Circle adventures in Orlando, Florida:

Now I lead zip lining adventures with my VIP Coaching Clients!

THE MORAL OF THE STORY

As we'll see throughout this book, your brain's job is *to keep you SAFE*, to make sure you don't die. Yet have you ever noticed that sometimes "playing it safe" can be the most DANGEROUS thing you can do?

Why? Because when you "play it safe" it means that not only will you miss out on life, you often won't allow yourself to grow and experience the best that life has to offer. So the next time you're faced with a choice like I had on that zip line platform, realize that you too have those same three choices:

Option 1: Try to go back to the way things were. (Sadly, this isn't possible.)

Option 2: Try to stay right where you are. (This isn't actually possible, either.)

Option 3: Take ACTION even in the face of fear.

It's true: As much as we would like to go back to the "good old days" or keep things from changing, those choices don't actually exist; because not only can we not go back to the past, but also life is changing far too rapidly to think that we can keep change from occurring. That's why the only actual choice is to *take ACTION, even in the face of fear.*

And in this book, I will show you exactly how to do just that.

THINKING IS FAR WORSE THAN DOING

Have you ever noticed that you can imagine things that never happen? Have you ever worried about things that never even occurred? I know I have. I've spent countless hours worrying about things that ultimately didn't even take place. As Mark Twain said, "I have known a great many troubles, most of which never happened."

That's why, if you're thinking about trying something new, it's nice to know that you're not the first person to try it. For example, have you ever looked up reviews of a restaurant or hotel you're considering going to? Have you ever read reviews on websites like Amazon or TripAdvisor before you purchased something on those sites?

We do this because we want the comfort of knowing that someone else has done and liked the thing we're thinking about trying. That's why, if other people have benefited from doing something, we're far more likely to "take the plunge" and try it for ourselves.

That's one reason this book includes many real-life case studies from my coaching clients, because reading their success stories may encourage you to give it a try too.

But let me back up for a second...

WHAT WE DO AT SUCCESSCLINIC.COM

In this book, I'm going to share with you my Power Habits® System that has helped my coaching clients—people just like you—to add more than $2.2 billion in sales since 1997. Yet first I'd like to share a little about what we do at my company, **SuccessClinic.com**.

At SuccessClinic.com, we help impact-driven entrepreneurs and business owners move from "impossible" to "I'm Possible."

What does that mean exactly? Well, when people like you hire me as their business coach or Power Habits® Mentor—or when businesses hire me to do keynote speeches or private workshops—each of them is facing what I call an "impossible barrier."

That means that they believe that it's "impossible" to achieve their dreams or reach their goals without some kind of huge sacrifice, drowning in "Information Overload," or working like a dog.

You see, for everyone it's different...

For example, maybe you're in a job that you hate, and you think it's "impossible" to launch your successful online business.

Maybe you love your job and you think it's "impossible" to create an additional stream of income (or two).

Maybe you're an entrepreneur with your own business, or a manager with many people who report to you…but you (and your business) are stuck, and you think it's "impossible" to get unstuck without driving yourself crazy.

Or maybe you think it's just "impossible" to really have a bigger *impact* on the world while making a great *income* and having *fun* doing it!

However, what I've found in more than 20 years of coaching and mentoring people just like you to achieve what they thought was "impossible" is this one simple, inescapable fact…

EVERYTHING YOU DESIRE HAPPENS WHEN YOU MOVE FROM "IMPOSSIBLE" TO "I'M POSSIBLE"

For instance, I used to believe it was "impossible" for me to make a lot of money, help a lot of people, and have a lot of fun. Yet today I get to do just that, every day of my life–and get handsomely paid for the privilege of doing it!

That's why our mission at SuccessClinic.com is to touch a billion lives through our work and help 100,000 entrepreneurs live the "Freedom Lifestyle" of their dreams.

Yes, it's an awe-inspiring mission—which is why it energizes and focuses us every day to serve as many people as possible who are ready to supercharge their results and enjoy the fruits of their labor without "tech overwhelm" and without "information overload."

Which means you're in the right place if you want to:

✓ Make a definitive difference in the world

✓ Have a genuine impact on the people you're here to serve

✓ Supercharge your ability to attract more wealth and abundance

✓ Enjoy more time off without the guilt

✓ Overcome the fear of failure so you can achieve more while working less

Because the great news is: You've already done most of the heavy lifting necessary to achieve your greatest dreams.

THE WORST DAY OF MY LIFE

You see, since starting SuccessClinic.com in my college dorm room in 1997, I've helped countless thousands of people just like you to reach their goals faster, easier, and with far less stress. Yet I wasn't always the "go-to guy" when it comes to success. In fact, I was anything but.

December 2006. I had just broken up with my girlfriend and moved back into my parent's house in Maine. As you can imagine, Maine in December is cold, and I felt as cold on the inside as the weather felt outside.

I FELT AS COLD ON THE INSIDE AS THE WEATHER WAS OUTSIDE.

At that point in my life, it dawned on me that I was completely broke and it just wasn't going to get any better unless I took ACTION. In fact, I remember that day vividly.

I was sitting in the corner of my parent's basement at this makeshift desk (it was actually a card table with a folding metal chair). I sat down with a pencil and a yellow legal pad and added up everything that I owed.

To my horror, I discovered that I was more than $40,000 in credit card debt and I was about to go under. I was beyond depressed. I felt completely worthless.

I felt like I hadn't even lived my life, yet there was no end in sight, no hope for a better tomorrow.

AT THAT MOMENT, I MADE A VOW

A promise to God that was like my own personal Declaration of Independence. I said to myself, *Enough! I will never, ever feel this way again. I'm going to solve this money problem or DIE TRYING!*

I swore that I would read every book and go through every course on marketing, success, how to make money, and I would also pick the brains of as many experts as I could find to discover the secrets of how to have real financial freedom.

In my journey, I stumbled on a secret formula to success, and I'm going to reveal it to you in this book. Yet even though today I've been very successful helping people just like you to achieve their dreams, I'm exactly like you are in so many ways.

I simply figured out a simple, step-by-step formula that anyone can use to move from "impossible" to "I'm Possible."

THE THREE MAJOR MILESTONES

In my 20-plus years of delivering keynote speeches, hosting private workshops, and coaching impact-driven individuals like you, I've come to realize that as you're building your business, you'll encounter three major milestones along the way.

As you can see from the illustration below, the first major milestone is when you make your first $10,000 in your business. (Of course, the first big hurdle is earning your first dollar online!) When you hit this first major milestone, it means your business stops being a "hobby" and you become an real ENTREPRENEUR.

The second major milestone is when you get to $100K a year, or about *$10,000 per month.* When you hit this level, your life really starts to change for the better—because now your mortgage is paid, you get to

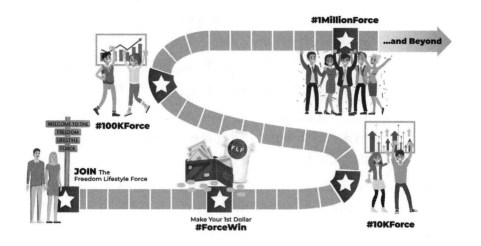

take your family on fun vacations, and your future looks more and more secure. Once you hit this level, you're considered an EXPERT.

The third major milestone occurs when your business hits $1 million and beyond. When you reach this milestone, now you're in the top 1 percent of all business owners, which means you're in rarefied air. Your house is paid for, you might even get a second home or vacation home, you no longer worry about bills, you're living 100 percent debt free, you're supporting causes that are truly important to you, and you're making a significant difference and having a major impact in the world. At this level, you're a true INFLUENCER.

WHO THIS IS FOR

That's why I designed The Power Habits® System with YOU in mind—whether you want to hit your first $10K in your business, you're working to get to $100K a year, or you're ready to make your first (or your next) million. That's because this System is tailored specifically for people who demand MORE:

✓ More RESULTS—because it empowers you to gain the recognition and the respect that you deserve.

✓ More SECURITY—because you'll finally have the time and money to do the things you want to do.

✓ More SELF-CONFIDENCE—because you'll come to realize that you're far stronger and more capable than you ever thought you were.

✓ And that means you'll have more ABILITY to overcome any obstacle that may be holding you back.

When individuals and organizations invest $100,000 or more for me to coach them, this is where we start. And in this book, I'll share my Power Habits® System with you, so you too can experience powerful results like these.

WHAT YOU CAN EXPECT

As we begin this journey together, I'd like to share with you just a few of the benefits you can expect to see as a result of using The Power Habits System.

In my experience coaching celebrities, professional athletes, CEOs, entrepreneurs, working moms, and busy people like you from around the world, if you follow the steps and install the habits that I describe in this book, you can expect measurable, even dramatic, improvements in these four areas:

1. **Your relationships will improve substantially.**

   Millions of people today are in relationships that are strained, unfulfilling, or broken. In fact, many people are finding that in today's fractured society, it's harder than ever to create meaningful, lasting relationships. That's why when you install The Power Habits in your life, your ability to create deep, bonding relationships with other people will be greatly improved.

2. **Your self-confidence will skyrocket.**

   Many people feel like they don't have much value outside of their job. By the same token, many people feel frustrated and underutilized at work. They know they have deep mines of energy, genius, and creativity that are barely being used. This creates a sense of frustration and sapping of energy that can make it difficult just to get through the day. By applying the principles you'll learn in this book, you'll gain a deeper understanding of your own value to yourself, your family and friends, your colleagues and coworkers, your customers, and the world. This will pay big dividends in increasing your self-esteem and self-confidence, no matter what the situation.

   YOU CAN EXPECT TO ENJOY THESE BENEFITS WHEN YOU FOLLOW THE POWER HABITS® SYSTEM.

3. **Your ability to succeed financially will increase significantly.**

   Would you like to attract more money and abundance into your life? How about doing work that fulfills you? Using these principles, many of my coaching clients have been able to start new businesses, get their first book published, find more fulfilling work, and grow their businesses by six, seven, and yes, even eight figures!

4. **You will experience a profound and lasting happiness.**

   When you live the life you know you were meant to live, it creates an inexorable feeling of excitement, energy, and sense

YOU CAN ELIMINATE THESE FEARS AND FRUSTRATIONS WHEN YOU FOLLOW MY SYSTEM.

of peace that can't be faked. As George Bernard Shaw said, "This is the true joy in life, the being used for a purpose recognized by yourself as a mighty one."

By the same token, if you're experiencing frustration, blocks, or pain in any of the following areas, you can expect to see remarkable improvements from applying The Power Habits System.

Now you might think that I'm hyping it up or exaggerating for effect. Yet, if anything, I'm *downplaying* it.

How can I say that? Because that statement is based on my firsthand experience of coaching and training tens of thousands of individuals, teams, companies, and organizations in more than 120 countries around the world in this System.

Therefore, here are four of the main frustrations that people, teams, and organizations have told me have been greatly reduced or even eliminated by using the principles in this System.

See if you can identify with any of these...

1. I often feel that when opportunity presents itself, I won't be in the right place or have the courage to take advantage of it.

2. I feel like there's a ceiling on my success, even though I've already spent tons of money on personal growth or professional development programs.

3. I know that I need to change some of my habits, but I don't know where to start, or what changes I need to make, or how to make those changes really last.

4. I've reached a certain level of success in my life and my business, but I know I'm capable of so much more.

28

Do any of these sound familiar to you?

If so, you're in the right place.

HERE'S WHAT THIS IS <u>NOT</u>

Are you as tired as I am of reading self-help books that say the same thing as every other self-help book?

Well, in this book, you're not going to find the same old clichés you've heard a million times before. Clichés like *just do it*, *think positive*, and *set your goals* are not allowed on these pages, any more than they're allowed in my keynote speeches, private workshops, or live seminars!

That's because, first of all, we've heard these tropes a million times before. Secondly, if clichés were enough to create success, then everyone would be successful! And third, for the last two decades, I've essentially made a living by making hamburgers out of the self-help industry's most sacred cows.

That's because instead of doing what all those other books and programs do (rely on clichés and empty promises), you and I are going to have a lot of fun re-examining many of the commonly-held beliefs and assumptions about success and looking at them with a brand-new perspective—a new perspective that, for countless thousands of people just like you around the world, has created dramatic, even life-changing improvements.

And in case you're looking for a program that says you don't have to do any work to create the results you want in life, you won't find that here either. (Rats!)

Yes, it's true: just like building a house, success in life and business doesn't simply

I ENJOY MAKING HAMBURGERS OUT OF SELF-HELP SACRED COWS.

happen by magic or by wishing or hoping. In fact, success in life and business takes this one thing: *Consistent ACTION in the face of fear.*

> **EVERYTHING YOU DESIRE IS ON THE OTHER SIDE OF FEAR.**

One of my favorite sayings is: "Everything you desire is on the other side of fear."

However, the great news is that if you follow my system, not only can you get results faster, easier, and with less effort than you're spending right now, but you'll also discover that you're more able to take consistent ACTION, even in the face of fear.

Now, it is true that some of my methods may seem a bit odd at first; yet that's exactly the point. Because, think about it: if you already had the lifestyle you desired and were as successful as you really wanted to be, you wouldn't need to try something different, now would you?

And I think you'll agree that if there were ever a time on this planet when we humans needed to apply a new level of thinking in order to create a world we can all live in sustainably, happily, and peacefully, it's RIGHT NOW.

So, let's get started right now, because...

You are not alone.

Noah St. John,
Inventor of Afformations®
Creator of Power Habits® Academy
Founder of Freedom Lifestyle Experience

TOP 10 WAYS TO GET
THE MOST FROM THIS BOOK

"Successful people aren't born that way.
They become successful by establishing the habit of
doing things unsuccessful people don't like to do."
— William Makepeace Thackeray

1. *Have the essential ingredient.* I know you're busy. Yes, I know you've got a million and one distractions pulling at you and your attention every second of every day. That's why, if you want to get the most out of this book, there's really only one essential ingredient you need.

However, without this essential ingredient, I can give you the best techniques in the world and they won't do a thing for you.

What is this essential ingredient? Simply this: *a clear, compelling desire to master The Power Habits® of Unconsciously Successful People.*

And how can you develop this desire? By constantly reminding yourself of how important these principles are to you. Imagine how mastering these Power Habits will empower you to live the life of your dreams—a richer, happier, more fulfilling life. Let that mental picture drive you toward your goals, using the principles I describe in this book.

2. As you read this book, *stop frequently to think about what you're reading.* I understand the temptation to skim through this book and get on to the next thing on your to-do list. Yet that's precisely the point: one of the reasons you probably feel "overwhelmed and overworked" is because you're not giving yourself time to THINK.

Think about how you're going to apply each of the 11 Power Habits in your life, your business, and your relationships. You may find that you're already doing some of these habits; yet some may be completely new to you. That's great—simply becoming aware of what's missing and what can be improved is one of the first steps to mastery.

3. *Read with a highlighter or pen in your hand.* As an author, I'm always overjoyed when loyal readers at my keynote speeches, private workshops, and live seminars show me their (my) books highlighted and covered with sticky notes! Because that proves that they have not simply read through my books; they also gave themselves the gift of PAYING ATTENTION.

Naturally, if you are reading the electronic version of this book, use the highlight function in the same manner. Be sure to include the date next to each highlighted passage so you can come back to this book later and see how far you've come!

4. *Use sticky notes or sticky flags.* In keeping with the previous suggestion, I suggest highlighting this book with either sticky notes or sticky flags so you'll be able to quickly find the pages and passages that have special meaning to you.

5. *Start a Power Habits® Study Group.* Because of the enormous outpouring of emotion and life-changing stories from loyal readers just like you from across the globe, I've created a Power Habits® Reader's Guide to accompany this book, for you to use in your book study group.

Starting a Power Habits Study Group will benefit you in several ways:

a. You'll empower yourself to install these habits in your daily life.

b. By socially committing in a public setting, you'll be less likely to fall back into old, disempowering habits.

c. You'll meet and network with success-minded people in your community.

Remember, your Power Habits Study Group can be online as well as offline—so you can use the power of the Internet to connect with other Power Habits fans around the world. See the *Recommended Resources* section at the back of this book for more information on how to get your free Power Habits® Reader's Guide.

6. *Keep a Power Habits® Journal.* These habits will only work for you if you practice them. And the best way to do that is to keep a Power Habits® Journal. Whether you like to write with pen and paper, on your laptop, or on your phone, the simple act of writing forces your brain to focus on the task at hand, which will in turn help you to install these Power Habits more quickly and easily.

Remember the ancient proverb: "The palest ink is stronger than the sharpest memory."

7. *Share your Power Habits stories with me.* I love to hear success stories from my loyal readers like you from around the world. No matter who you are or where you're from, I invite you to share your story with me on our main website: **NoahStJohn.com**.

On our site, you'll find photos, videos, and success stories posted by people from around the world who have used my proven methods to change their lives. You'll feel inspired reading about other people's experiences and how they overcame life's challenges using these principles.

Plus, my amazing Client Success Team and I are here to help you any time you have questions, need support, or would like to go to the next level with your personal and/or business growth.

You can find out more by visiting our other websites, including **WorkingwithNoah.com** and **ShopNoahStJohn.com** for access to home-study programs, personal coaching, mastermind groups, and our transformational live events.

8. *Do you like to win prizes? Do this!* Just upload a selfie of yourself holding one of my books and hashtag it **#NoahStJohn** and tag me **@noahstjohn**.

Here's all you have to do...

1. Take a selfie of yourself holding one of my books (like the one you're holding right now!)

2. Upload your selfie to your Facebook and/or Instagram account.

3. (Very important) Hashtag me **#NoahStJohn** and tag **@noahstjohn**.

We pick a new winner every month!

You only need to enter once and you'll have a chance to win every single month.

9. *Take part in the #PowerHabitsChallenge.* Each chapter of Part 2 of this book includes a The Power Habits Challenge, where I encourage you to do one thing related to that chapter's Power Habit and post it on social media using the hashtag #PowerHabitsChallenge.

WANT TO WIN COOL PRIZES? UPLOAD A SELFIE OF YOURSELF HOLDING ONE OF MY BOOKS!

TAKE PART IN THE #POWERHABITSCHALLENGE.

Taking part in The Power Habits Challenge will increase your self-confidence and empower you to install these habits because you won't be doing it alone. You'll also be amazed at how doing such a simple thing can make such a big difference in your life.

And finally...

10. *Come to one of our live events.* As great as reading and sharing on social media are, there's simply no substitute for being there LIVE. That's because, when we get together at our live workshops and mastermind groups, something happens that's simply magical. (For example, we've literally had people do million-dollar deals at my live events!)

TO GET THE MOST FROM THIS TEACHING, COME TO ONE OF OUR LIVE EVENTS.

In addition, you'll meet and network with like-minded people, many of whom can become lifelong friends, colleagues, and joint venture partners. You'll also get the chance to work with me directly as well as with my Power Habits® Certified Coaches, so you can get the help you need to move from "impossible" to "I'm Possible."

In addition, attending one of our live events will make it far easier for you to install these new, empowering habits—which means you'll be able to reach your goals faster, easier, and with far less effort than ever before. Visit **FreedomLifeX.com** for more information on upcoming dates and locations.

Finally, connect with me through our main website **NoahStJohn. com** and share your Power Habits success story with me—because I'd love to see *your* success story in one of my upcoming books!

PART 1

WHY POWER HABITS®?

CHAPTER 1

THE HIDDEN CONNECTION BETWEEN HABITS AND SUCCESS

"Powerful indeed is the empire of habit."
— Publilius Syrus

Would you like to change anything in your life? For example, would you like to have...

✓ More control over your life choices

✓ More free time to spend with your family

✓ A more fulfilling career

✓ More money to enjoy the good things in life

✓ More vibrant health and lower stress

✓ Happier relationships

✓ Greater satisfaction at work

✓ A more abundant lifestyle

Well of course you would—that's why you're reading this book!

However, my guess is that this is not the first book of this kind you've read. (If it is, welcome to The Power Habits® Revolution!)

I suspect that you've tried many things to achieve results like the ones I just listed. In fact, if you're like the thousands of clients I've worked with at our seminars and in our coaching and mastermind groups, you've probably tried lots and lots of things.

WHAT HAVE YOU TRIED SO FAR?

So here's your first exercise, and it's an easy one. (Thank goodness!)

Place a checkmark (either written or mental) next to the things on the list below that you've tried in the past in order to get the results like the ones listed above.

"So far, I've tried...

❑ Reading self-help books

❑ Buying personal growth programs

❑ Attending conferences and seminars

❑ Starting a new diet or exercise program

❑ Joining a gym

❑ Writing down your goals

❑ Doing vision boards

❑ Practicing positive thinking

Now my guess is that you've already tried many or even all of these methods in order to create the positive changes you desire to see in your life. So, the question is, have these methods worked to create the life you truly desire? And if not, why not?

The simple fact is that millions of people who've tried all of these methods—many of whom have spent *tens or even hundreds of thousands of dollars* on these methods—are still NOT living the lifestyle they want.

(And I should know, because these are the people who hire me to coach them, do private workshops, train their organizations, and who come to my live seminars and keynote speeches.)

There are several possible answers to this question of "Why haven't these methods worked?" For example:

1. The methods are flawed.

2. The people who do them don't do them right.

3. There's something the "gurus" didn't tell us.

After coaching and training tens of thousands of people just like you from around the globe, I've found that the main reason most people don't live the life they desire is, surprisingly, a combination of all three of these things. However, not in the way you might think.

Let me explain…

THE TWO THINGS THAT CREATE YOUR LIFE

What I'm about to show you is one of the reasons that my coaching clients have added more than $2.2 billion in sales since 1997.

I know that's a bold statement. However, once you begin to understand the hidden connection between habits and success, everything will start to fall into place for you.

As surprising as it may seem, your life is created by just two things: the quality of your communication with the world *inside* of you and the quality of your communication with the world *outside* of you.

Your communication with the world inside of you is what I call **your Inner Game.** The Inner Game deals with everything that happens in your life in the space between your ears that you can't see directly, but whose EFFECTS you see everywhere.

YOUR LIFE IS CREATED BY THESE TWO THINGS.

For example, you can't see your beliefs, values, desires, thoughts, or decisions. Those things you can't see directly, but you see the EFFECTS of them everywhere in your life. In fact, I argue that you see the effects of your Inner Game AS your life.

Here's another example: in my keynote speeches, private workshops, and live seminars, I often ask my audience members a simple question: "Please tell me one area of your life that is NOT affected by your beliefs."

Of course, people look at each other and ponder the question in silence, trying to come up with an area of their lives that is NOT affected by their beliefs, i.e., their Inner Game.

For instance, how about your health? Is your health affected by your beliefs? (Of course.)

Your money? Your career? Are those affected by your beliefs? (Without question.)

Your relationships—both personal and professional? (No doubt.)

What you do with your free time? Whom you spend your time with? (Certainly.)

So you can see that your Inner Game absolutely affects every single thing you do—every aspect of your life, both personally and professionally.

But what about the other aspect—the part of your life that you CAN see directly?

Your communication with the world outside of you is what I call **your Outer Game**. These are the things you CAN see directly and that absolutely ALSO affect your life.

For example, your Outer Game consists of things like your habits, lifestyle, actions, behaviors, systems, and strategies. Why are they called the Outer Game? Because they're right in front of you; you can see them right in front of your face.

HOW THIS PLAYS OUT IN YOUR LIFE

For instance, let's look at your health. How is your health affected by your Inner Game and Outer Game?

Well, your Inner Game regarding your health includes things like:

- ✓ How you talk to yourself about your weight
- ✓ What you say to yourself about your body
- ✓ What you believe is possible regarding your health
- ✓ What you believe is NOT possible regarding your health
- ✓ How soon you will quit when things get tough regarding your health
- ✓ ...and so on.

Keep in mind that you can't see any of these things directly. There's no flashing sign above your head that says: "Here's what I'm thinking about my body right now!"

Or is there...?

Why do I say it like that? Because the fact is that your Outer Game regarding your health includes things like:

- ✓ What you eat

✓ What you don't eat

✓ When you eat

✓ How often you eat (or don't)

✓ How often you exercise (or don't)

✓ The fact that you smoke or drink alcohol (or don't)

✓ ...and so forth.

Are you starting to see the hidden connection between your habits and your success? Because the truth is that:

1. Your Inner Game and Outer Game are always operating together, regardless of whether or not you're aware of that fact.

2. Most people are only focused on one aspect of their lives, and that's never going to work.

That's because it is only when you MASTER your Inner Game and your Outer Game that you have the thing called Success—as shown in the diagram on the next page.

IGNORE THIS AT YOUR PERIL

Let's suppose you want to make more money (who doesn't?). And let's also suppose that you've been listening to those "gurus" who tell you that "all you have to do is work on your mindset" and you'll be successful.

So you gamely work on your mindset—you watch your thoughts, try to eliminate all "negative thinking" from your mind, meditate, practice gratitude, and all the other things they tell you to do.

Yet for some reason, your money is not increasing. In fact, it's actually *decreasing!*

INNER GAME OUTER GAME

Beliefs	S	Habits
Values	U	Lifestyle
Desires	C	Actions
Thoughts	C	Behaviors
Priorities	E	Systems
Decisions	S	Strategies
	S	

But how could this happen? If you focus all your time, money, and effort on improving your Inner Game, surely you'll succeed, right?

Well, it would be great if that were true. The only problem, however, is that it never works that way.

WHAT IF YOU ONLY FOCUS ON ONE OF THESE?

To go back to our health example, if this were true, all we'd have to do is "think positive" and we could sit around all day, eating junk food and never exercising—and we'd all have six-pack abs and be in perfect shape!

To use the relationship example, if this worked, we could think nice thoughts about our partner while simultaneously shaming

44

them, talking badly about them, griping and complaining about them, and never showing gratitude—and expect to have a happy relationship!

When I make it as simple as that, it's pretty clear that focusing on your Inner Game alone is not enough to create Success—whether in your health, your wealth, your relationships, or your business.

So it's not enough to work on your Inner Game. But what if we work only on our Outer Game?

I bet you can think of many people who seem to work only on their Outer Game while ignoring their Inner Game. In fact, we see examples like this all the time—people who have all the trappings of success (fame, fortune, status, possessions, etc.) yet either are very unhappy or end up losing it.

Why does this happen? Because they didn't master their Inner Game, the true foundation for long-term success.

YOU MUST MASTER BOTH YOUR INNER GAME AND OUTER GAME IF YOU WANT TO SUCCEED.

Elvis Presley. John Belushi. River Phoenix. Andy Gibb. Chris Farley. John Candy. Janis Joplin. Jimi Hendrix. Jim Morrison. Robin Williams.

The fact is, the pages of history (and on the Internet today) are littered with people who had the appearance of success but ended up losing everything because they hadn't mastered their Inner Game.

Imagine if you had a house with no electricity. That house is not much fun to live in, because you can't do most of the things we take for granted every day (like watch TV, use the Internet, microwave your breakfast, etc.).

But guess what? While you can't see electricity, you definitely see the *effects* of it. That's what your Inner Game is like.

Meanwhile, without your Outer Game, you don't have a house in the first place! You're living on a park bench somewhere. That would suck too.

That's why we have to master both our Inner Game and Outer Game in order to have the thing called Success.

MY $2.2 BILLION PROOF

As I've shared with you previously, my clients and I have collectively grown our businesses by more than $2.2 BILLION as a result of my teachings. That means that I've helped my clients—people just like you from around the world—to add six, seven, and yes, even eight figures to their businesses.

Yet here's something you might not expect: that multi-billion-dollar growth largely occurred because of what I help my clients do in their *Inner Game.*

NINETY PERCENT OF SUCCESS IS MASTERING YOUR INNER GAME.

Based on my experience in working with thousands of clients over the last two decades, 90 percent of your success comes from your Inner Game, while only 10 percent comes from your Outer Game.

Now that might not be what you expected—and you may not even believe it right now. That's because it's precisely the opposite of what all those "gurus" are teaching out there.

For example, I bet you've taken lots of courses on marketing, sales, and how to grow your business. And of course, that's important. As I mentioned, you can't have success in business without that kind of training.

However, *all of that is Outer Game.* And as I just showed you, only when you combine Inner Game Mastery with Outer Game Systems do you get to enjoy the phenomenon called SUCCESS.

YOUR SUCCESS WILL COME MUCH FASTER AND LAST LONGER WHEN YOU FOLLOW MY SYSTEM.

In fact, once you follow The Power Habits® System, your success will not only come much faster, it will last much longer and be far more satisfying too.

The truth is, most of the people who hire me to coach or train them, or hire me to speak at seminars and conferences, had previously spent tens or even hundreds of thousands of dollars on Outer Game training. Yet because no one had been able to show them how to master their Inner Game, they were still STUCK.

In fact, until now, you may not have even realized that there IS a formula for mastering your Inner Game. And that's exactly what The Power Habits® System does. When you follow my System, you'll master your Inner Game of Success...

Which means you'll stop stopping yourself from success...

And that means you're going to allow yourself to succeed at higher levels than ever before.

I hope that makes you as excited to learn my System as I am to teach it to you!

NOAH'S NOTES (IN A NUTSHELL)

1. Most people want to improve one or more areas of their lives: health, money, business, relationships.

2. Most people, especially the ones reading this book, have tried a multitude of ways to improve their lives and get results.

3. Yet most people remain frustrated, overwhelmed, or just stuck. That's because what they tried was incomplete or just plain wrong.

4. Your life is determined by just two things: the quality of your communication with the world *inside* you and the quality of your communication with the world *outside* you. These are called your **Inner Game** and **Outer Game**, respectively.

5. When you focus only on either your Inner Game or your Outer Game, it's going to be very difficult, if not impossible, for you to enjoy long-term, lasting success.

6. Based on more than two decades of research and experience, 90 percent of an individual's success is comprised of Inner Game Mastery, while only 10 percent is Outer Game Systems.

7. The primary reason for my clients collectively adding more than $2.2 billion in revenue growth is because they followed my Power Habits® System—a proven, step-by-step formula to master both the Inner Game and Outer Game of Success.

CHAPTER 2

HOW WE STOP OURSELVES FROM SUCCESS—AND WHY

"Winning is a habit. Unfortunately, so is losing."
— Vince Lombardi

Imagine you wanted to build a house. Where would you start? What's the first thing you would do?

Well, you'd probably start by deciding where you want to live. Do you want to live near the ocean or up in the mountains? On a lake or close to the best shopping areas? In what state, city, and neighborhood do you want to build your house?

Let's say you've decided where you want to live. What would you do next?

Perhaps your next step would be to decide on the size and general design of your new house. You'd put a lot of thought into this, because (presumably) you'll be spending the next several years in this house, if not longer. So you'd spend a great deal of time and attention on making sure it's the house you really want.

At this point, unless you're an architect by trade, you'd probably want to hire an architect to help you build your dream house. Why? Because there is a heck of a lot that goes into building a house—which means there's a lot that can go wrong.

That's why architects (the good ones, certainly) have spent years mastering their craft. That's also why, when you hire a good architect, you're fairly certain that they're not going to steer you in the wrong direction—and that the end result will be something you're pleased with and you and your family will enjoy.

I think you'd agree that what I just described is a typical way to build a house. Yet isn't it ironic that that is NOT the way most people live their lives?

Let me explain...

Imagine that you're back at the beginning, and you want to build a house. So you get up in the morning and say, "Hey, I think I want to build a house!"

And you go, "Hmm, what's a house made of?"

And you think, *I know—wood!*

So you go to the hardware store and order some boards of wood.

Then you go, "How the heck do you put these things together?"

And you figure, *Nails! I'm going to use nails!*

So you buy some nails and then you go, "What should I use to drive these nails into these boards?"

I know—a hammer!

So you grab a hammer and some nails, and you start nailing boards together.

And you say to yourself, *"I bet if I work really hard, a house is going to show up!"*

WHAT'S WRONG HERE?

So what would you say is wrong with this method?

Exactly—EVERYTHING!

1. You don't have a **plan**.

2. You don't have a **blueprint**.

3. You don't have a **framework**.

4. You don't have **anyone there to help you**.

5. Worst of all... *you have no idea what you're doing!*

The sad truth is that, while no one would ever dream of building a house like this... *millions of people are living their lives in exactly this way.*

1. They don't have a **plan**.

2. They don't have a **blueprint**.

3. They don't have a **framework**.

4. They don't have **anyone there to help them**.

5. Worst of all... *they have no idea how to get out of this situation!*

Can you relate to this analogy?

✓ Have you been busy "slapping boards together"—trying to fix your business, your organization, your team—without really having a cohesive, step-by-step plan, blueprint, or framework?

✓ Have you spent tens of thousands of dollars (or more) trying to figure out new and better way to nail boards together, hoping a house shows up?

✓ Are you frustrated because, even after all this time, money, and effort spent, you're still not "living in your dream home"?

This simple analogy explains why people, teams, organizations, and companies hire me to coach them, do private workshops, or train their people—because they've ended up with a "house" (business/life/ organization) that's pretty "drafty"—that is, constructed without a proper plan, blueprint, or framework.

And it's not because they're not working hard, or not dedicated or smart enough. It's because no one has taken the time to show them the proper *blueprint for success*.

WHY YOU NEED A BLUEPRINT

WITHOUT A PROPER BLUEPRINT, YOUR "HOUSE" IS GOING TO BE PRETTY DRAFTY.

Based on the analogy above, it's clear that the best way to build a house is to *start with a blueprint*. That's also one of the main reasons you hire an architect if you want to ensure that your house is built properly. Why? Because an architect is someone who has not just studied "how to build a house" but someone who also has the *expertise* and *knowledge* of having successfully done it many, many times before.

Now assuming you choose to go the second way—that is, to stop slapping boards together and hire someone to help you build your dream home—what's the first question your architect is going to ask you?

Exactly: the first question your architect will ask you is: "What kind of house do you want?"

For example:

✓ How many bedrooms do you want?

✓ Do you want a two- or three-car garage?

✓ What do your want in your kitchen?

✓ Do you want tile or marble?

✓ How big do you want the living room?

✓ And so on.

GETTING A PLAN IS FAR LESS EXPENSIVE THAN NOT HAVING ONE.

The point is, there are A LOT of decisions that go into building your dream home. Yet the reality is that *it's YOUR dream home.*

YOU are the one who's going to live there. That's why it had better be the house that YOU really desire to live in—not someone else's idea for you. (We'll examine this concept further in the chapter on *Goal Replacement Surgery.*)

So now you have your "dream home blueprint." What happens next?

What happens next is that you simply *follow the plan.* For example, each day when you start to work on your house, you simply look at the plan and go, "What needs to get done today?"

Because it's right there in front of you, every step of the way.

And it sure is easier, a lot less stressful, and ultimately **FAR LESS EXPENSIVE in time, money, and effort** than running around, slapping boards together, and hoping a house shows up!

STOP STRUGGLING NOW

Most of the people who come to me have been working really hard, just like I was. Struggling, spending lots of money, putting in lots of time and energy... but they still don't have their dream home.

That's where this System comes into play. Why? Because it's a blueprint. A framework. It's a step-by-step, fill-in-the-blank series of checklists.

No more guessing.

No more fear.

No more lack.

No more wondering, "What am I supposed to be doing today?"

It's all in the System.

Keep reading to see why...

8

CHAPTER 3

THE PROVEN SECRET TO MORE WEALTH AND HAPPINESS

"Habit is stronger than reason."
— George Santayana

I have the privilege of coaching celebrities, athletes, CEOs, entrepreneurs, and hardworking people just like you from around the world. I'm also honored to give keynote presentations and lead private workshops and life-changing seminars that help people, teams, and organizations go from mere *information* to genuine *transformation*.

One of my teachings that's had a profound effect on my coaching clients and live event audiences is what I'm about to share with you. In fact, I even had one woman at one of my seminars tell me that she was going to have the image I'm about to show you tattooed on her shoulder!

While you may not want to go that far, I hope that what I'm about to show you will make a profound difference for you too.

Now one of the first questions I ask my coaching clients is, "Why are you in business?" And I get many answers to that question...

I need to provide for my family.

> **FOCUS ON WHAT CAUSES MONEY AND HAPPINESS AND YOU'LL HAVE MORE OF BOTH.**

I want to make a lot of money.

I want to change the world.

I want to make a difference.

I hate my job.

I have a dream to own my own company.

These are just a few of the most common answers. However, when you boil it down, the essential answer to the question of why you are in business is...

You want more INCOME and you want more HAPPINESS.

Now it seems logical that if you want more income and more happiness, you should simply focus on getting more of those things. Right?

And that's what most people do—focus on *trying to make money* and *trying to be happier*. And while there's nothing wrong with that, there's just one teensy problem...

It doesn't work.

Why not? Because both money and happiness are the RESULTS of other things.

Therefore, rather than focusing on trying to make more money and trying to be happier (which are results or outcomes), the truth is that we need to focus on **what causes money (income)** and **what causes happiness**.

THE INCOME-HAPPINESS SCALE

Now let me introduce you to that famous illustration that has created so many "Aha!" moments for my coaching clients and audience members: **The Income-Happiness Scale**.

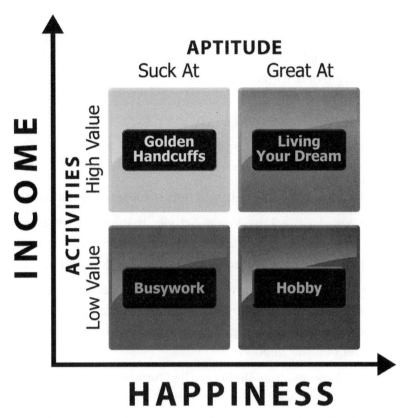

Copyright © Noah St. John and Success Clinic International—income happiness

As you can see in the illustration above, we have **Income** (money) going up the vertical axis and **Happiness** going across the horizontal axis. The more money you make, the more you go up the vertical axis; and the happier you are, the more you go across the horizontal axis.

There are two main factors that cause Income and Happiness: **Activities** and **Aptitude**. *Activities* are the things that you do every day—what you actually do with the minutes and hours of your day.

There are two kinds of Activities you can do each day: **Low-Value Activities** and **High-Value Activities**.

Aptitude means two things: how good you are at doing a certain Activity and how much you enjoy doing it. Therefore, there are two aspects of Aptitude: things you **Suck At** (and don't enjoy doing) and things you're **Great At** (and enjoy doing).

THE HOBBY QUADRANT

Let's start in the lower right-hand corner of the Income-Happiness Scale.

When you have a Low-Value Activity that you're Great At (and you enjoy), you have what's called a **Hobby**. What's the definition of a Hobby? It's something you enjoy doing that you don't get paid to do.

Naturally, there's nothing wrong with having hobbies. In fact, all of us should take the time to enjoy our hobbies—for example, activities like golf, tennis, gardening, sewing, reading, kayaking, ballroom dancing, or any number of other hobbies.

There is, however, one slight problem here, and it comes when I ask my clients a simple yet profound question: *Do you own a business, or do you own a hobby?*

How can you tell the difference? Simple. With a hobby, you're having fun—see how it's high on the Happiness axis—yet you're not making much (or any) money—see how it's low on the Income axis.

As it relates to your business, that's why it's crucial to ask yourself whether you *own a business* or if you *own a hobby.*

THE BUSYWORK QUADRANT

Moving to our lower left quadrant, we have *Low-Value Activities* that you *Suck At* (and don't enjoy). That's what I call **Busywork**.

We live in a world of infinite distractions. You can watch cat videos on YouTube until the end of time. You can waste countless hours on social media. Or you can simply spend the days of your life doing Activities that don't grow your business and don't give you either the Income or the Happiness you want.

TIME IS THE ONE RESOURCE THAT CAN NEVER BE REPLACED.

Notice that in the Busywork quadrant, your Activities aren't producing much money, and you're not enjoying them either. So you don't even get the benefit of having a Hobby. In fact, one of my clients told me on one of our coaching calls, "Noah, I *own* a Busywork!"

Do YOU *"own a Busywork"*? Or are you just spending too much of your valuable time there?

Why is this such an important question to ask? Because, as we'll discuss throughout this book, TIME is the one resource that can never be replaced!

THE GOLDEN HANDCUFFS

Moving to our upper left quadrant, we have *High-Value Activities* that you *Suck At* (and don't enjoy). That's what I call the **Golden Handcuffs**. Let me tell you a story to illustrate this quadrant.

We frequently have married couples attend my transformational live events, because of our "Buy 1, Bring a Guest FREE" policy. Recently, a real estate professional named Lauren brought her husband Dan to one of my live events. Before either of them said a word, it was clear by their body language that Lauren had to practically drag Dan to attend the seminar!

While he didn't say anything, Dan's body language was very clear: *What am I doing here? I don't want to be here. How can I get out of this?* (By the way, this is a common phenomenon from husbands who are "dragged" by their spouses to personal growth seminars!)

I could tell just by looking at Dan that he didn't really want to be there. I actually wondered how long he was going to last before he ducked out of the room.

I took a deep breath and started with my teaching. And then something amazing happened…

Within the first 20 minutes, Dan uncrossed his arms. Then he started leaning forward in his chair (a sure sign that someone is interested in what you're saying). Then his jaw dropped open as if he were hearing things that he'd never heard before. Then he started taking notes. Then he started taking A LOT of notes!

By the end of the event, Lauren and Dan had signed up for my VIP Coaching program, where I work with entrepreneurs at a very high level to help them build a multiple six- or seven-figure "Dream Lifestyle" business.

> **LIVING YOUR DREAM IS LIKE GOING TO HEAVEN WITHOUT THE INCONVENIENCE OF DYING.**

Dan told me afterwards that one of the reasons they decided to join my coaching program was because *he had been living in the Golden Handcuffs quadrant.* He had been working in a situation where he was making good money, but he hated his job. He was unhappy and frequently sick, and he had to spend a lot of time away from his family. But he felt that he couldn't leave that job because he had to take care of his family.

Have you ever been in a situation like that— where you're making good money but are unhappy and unfulfilled? That's why it's called the "Golden" Handcuffs—because it's awfully hard to leave a job that pays well, even if you hate it.

LIVING YOUR DREAM

And finally, we get to the place where we all want to go: where you are doing *High-Value Activities* that you're *Great At* (and that you enjoy doing). That's where you're in the quadrant I call **Living Your Dream**.

Why do we call it *Living Your Dream?* Because when you're doing High-Value Activities that you're Great At AND that you love doing, you're not only living your dream…

It's like going to heaven without the inconvenience of dying!

When you're Living Your Dream, notice what's happening to your Income. Your Income is going up, but your Happiness is going up too. In fact, *there is no limit* to the amount of Income you can create and *no limit* to the amount of Happiness you can experience. Pretty cool, huh?

The fact is, you too CAN Live Your Dream.

I know, I know…it sounds "impossible."

Yet I've seen it happen in my own life—in fact, I'm blessed to experience it every day! However, I also see it in the lives of my coaching clients and mastermind students every day as well, when they choose to follow my System.

In fact, that's exactly what happened to Dan. He decided to leave the job he hated and start his own landscaping company. Now he's making great money doing what he loves to do. Plus, he gets to spend time outdoors (which he loves), and he also gets to spend more time with his family, which gives him a great deal of happiness and fulfillment.

Yes, this truly IS possible for **YOU** too!

This is one of the wonderful benefits you can enjoy when you follow my Power Habits System, because not only will you be making more money, you'll also be helping more people and having a lot more fun.

It's true: when you're helping people and getting paid to share your message, life becomes amazingly rich, fulfilling, and fun!

But what happens when we stop ourselves from reaching the level of success we're capable of? Well, it's kind of like this…

CHAPTER 4

ARE YOU DRIVING DOWN THE ROAD OF LIFE WITH ONE FOOT ON THE BRAKE?

"It is easier to prevent bad habits than to break them."
— Benjamin Franklin

Imagine that you want to take a road trip and drive from Los Angeles to New York. You've got a nice reliable car that you believe will enable you to get where you want to go. You do all the things necessary to prepare for your trip: you pack, plan your route, determine how long it's going to take, and decide on how far you'd like to go each day and the sights you'd like to see along the way.

On the first day of your trip, you start driving on the highway toward your destination. You're thinking positively; you're motivated, and you can't wait to start your journey. So, naturally, you press down on the gas pedal in order to go toward your destination (or goal).

However, unbeknownst to you, at the same time you have one foot on the gas—you've developed the unconscious habit of driving *with your other foot on the brake!*

So here you are, driving along the highway, attempting to reach your goal. And you're wondering why the other drivers keep passing you, honking their horns and making interesting hand gestures.

Hmmm, you think. *I wonder why I'm not going very fast....*

Now, if you're driving down the road with one foot on the brake and one foot on the gas, how long do you think it's going to take to reach your destination? Exactly—it's going to take you *a long, long, long time to get there.*

After a while, you start to notice that you're not reaching your goals as fast as you thought you were going to. So naturally, you start to search for a solution—a way to reach your destination (goal) faster.

You stop for a break and ask someone who seems to be reaching their goals because, you know, they look cool.

This cool-looking person says to you, "You know what you need? You should use a more expensive type of gas. I bought this really expensive gas and it worked great for me. That's what you should do."

So you say, "Okay," pull your car into the gas station, and fill your tank with the most expensive high-octane gas you can find. Then you get back in your car and get back on the highway.

But guess what? Because you're still (unconsciously) doing the habit of *driving with one foot on the brake,* you're still not making much progress.

So you figure maybe the gas wasn't the issue and ask someone else what they think the problem is. This other person says to you, "You know what you need? You should get a new set of tires. I bought these really expensive tires and they work great for me. That's what you should do."

So you say, "Okay," go to the nearest tire store, buy the most expensive tires they have, and get back on the highway.

But guess what? Because you're still doing the same habit of driving with one foot on the brake, you're still not reaching your destination (goal) very fast.

YOU'VE DEVELOPED THE UNCONSCIOUS HABIT OF DRIVING WITH ONE FOOT ON THE BRAKE.

Finally, you seek out the coolest-looking person you can find and ask them what you should do. And this really cool person says, "You know what you need? You should get a new car. I bought this really expensive new car and it worked great for me. That's what you should do."

So you reluctantly say, "Okay," trade in your nice reliable car, and spend a ton of your hard-earned money buying an expensive new car. And thinking positively, but with less money in your bank account, you get back on the highway of life.

Yet even after all this time, money, and effort you've spent—even after trying all these different strategies and methods—because no one took the time to show you the real problem, which was simply the fact that *you have developed the habit of driving with one foot on the brake and one foot on the gas,* you end up not reaching your goals, not fulfilling your destiny, and feeling so frustrated that you eventually give up on your dreams.

Therefore, let me ask you a question: If buying more expensive gas, more expensive tires, and even a brand-new car isn't going to get you where you want to go, shouldn't you *do whatever it takes* to do these two things:

First, learn why you developed the habit of driving with your foot on the brake in the first place; and second, learn how to replace that very costly habit with **more productive habits**—so you can reach your goals faster, easier, and with far less effort!

WHY YOU HAVE YOUR FOOT ON THE BRAKE

STOP DRIVING DOWN THE ROAD OF LIFE WITH ONE FOOT ON THE BRAKE.

In human terms, what does it mean to have your foot on the brake? It means that at the very same time that you really desire to change your life, reach your goals, and fulfill your destiny, you're also *unconsciously engaging in habits* that are preventing you from doing that very thing.

Why, then, would we have our foot on the brake in the first place?

To answer that question, we first have to look at what you're going after in the first place. We humans are goal-oriented organisms. We see something we desire, and we decide to go after it.

Simply put, a *goal* is someplace you want to get to—like in the driving example above. Whether it's a new level of income, starting your business, growing your business, losing weight, finding your soulmate, getting your first book published—these are all examples of goals that I've helped people just like you to attain.

So the question is, are your current habits moving you *toward* your goals, or are they *stopping you* from reaching them?

For example, let's say that one of your goals is to get in shape, lose weight, and live a healthier lifestyle. That's where you want to go—your destination. So, what would some habits be that would move you *toward* that goal?

Well, you know that drinking water throughout the day will dramatically improve your health and help you lose weight. So, drinking water would be an example of a habit that would be like "stepping on the gas"—because it's a habit that would move you *toward* your stated goal.

8

However, let's say that right now, instead of the habit of drinking water throughout the day, you instead have developed the habit of drinking soda throughout the day. And since drinking soda does not help you lose weight, I think we can agree that drinking soda is a great example of "keeping your foot on the brake."

So here you have two opposing forces: the force of your "foot on the gas"—your conscious desire to lose weight—and the force of your other "foot on the brake"—which is your habit of drinking soda. Which force or habit do you think is going to win?

The answer is: whichever habit has the most traction.

To illustrate this principle, consider this old parable:

> One evening an old Cherokee told his grandson about a battle that goes on inside people.
>
> He said, "My son, the battle is between two 'wolves' inside us all.
>
> "One is Evil. It is anger, envy, jealousy, sorrow, regret, greed, arrogance, self-pity, guilt, resentment, inferiority, lies, false pride, superiority, and ego.
>
> "The other is good. It is joy, peace, love, hope, serenity, humility, kindness, benevolence, empathy, generosity, truth, compassion, and faith."
>
> The grandson thought about it for a moment, then asked his grandfather: "Which wolf wins?"
>
> The old Cherokee replied, "The one you feed."

THE HABIT WITH THE MOST TRACTION IS GOING TO WIN.

The point is, all of us have these two opposing forces inside of us: the loving and

PROCRASTINATION IS ONE OF THE COSTLIEST UNPRODUCTIVE HABITS.

giving part—you could call it your *Higher Self* or *Authentic Self*—and the greedy, lustful, aggressive part—you could call it your *Lower Self* or *Negative Reflection*.

Therefore, when we talk about habits, we're really talking about two different kinds of habits. At SuccessClinic.com, we don't use the terms "good habits" and "bad habits" because when people try to break so-called "bad" habits, it's often very difficult.

That's why in my keynote speeches and private workshops, as well as with my coaching clients and mastermind students, we use the terms *productive habits* and *unproductive habits*. Here's how it works…

PRODUCTIVE VS. UNPRODUCTIVE HABITS

At SuccessClinic.com, we describe *productive habits* as those that move you *toward* your desired goal or destination. By the same token, *unproductive habits* are those that *stop you, slow you down,* or actually *prevent you* from reaching your desired goal or destination.

For example, let's say you have a project that's due at work. You know you should work on the project, yet for some reason you keep putting it off. You keep finding other things to do rather than work on this project that's due.

When you do this, you're doing the habit called *procrastinating*. When you procrastinate, you are putting your "foot on the brake," because doing this habit is stopping you from reaching your destination, which is to finish the project.

How does the habit of procrastination show up in your life? For one thing, you'll probably keep finding other things to do—other reasons to do Busywork-type activities—and not work on the project. Then, at the last minute, when you know the deadline is looming and you just can't put it off anymore… that's when you suddenly step on the gas!

You "put the pedal to the metal," sweat bullets, and somehow complete the project just in time. But inside, you know it's probably not your best work. The sad thing is, your boss probably knows it, and your co-workers probably know it too.

YOU know it's not your best work. **YOU** know that it didn't have to be this way. So you promise yourself that you won't do it again.

However, the next time a big project is due—or you have to make that important phone call, write that article or blog post, shoot that video, or whatever the project might be—you find yourself going right back to the old, familiar habit of procrastinating, not doing your best work, and beating yourself up again afterwards.

Why, then, would you continue to do habits such as these—habits that you absolutely know do NOT contribute to your happiness, wealth, and well-being?

THE HABIT LOOP

Just as before, in order to answer this question, we must first ask a deeper question: *What exactly are habits, and how are they formed in the first place?*

To answer this question, let's turn to the field of neuroscience, the study of the human brain and its function, and see how it applies to our everyday lives.

> WHEN YOU PROCRASTINATE, YOU KNOW IT DOESN'T HAVE TO BE THIS WAY— BUT YOU DON'T SEE A WAY OUT.

Let's go back to our goal of losing weight and the desire to live a healthier lifestyle. That's your *destination,* and you know consciously that in order to reach your destination, you need to change your daily habits—for example, drink more water and less soda.

The problem is, even though you know *consciously* that's what you should do, it's hard to do, because you're so used to drinking soda throughout the day. What you've probably tried to do to change this habit is to use your **willpower**.

YOUR HABITS ARE FORMED BY THE HABIT LOOP.

Willpower is just what it sounds like—using the power of your *conscious will* to force yourself to do something you don't want to do. Therefore, willpower is essentially *using your conscious mind* to fight your subconscious habits.

And while you were probably able to make some changes for a short time using willpower, after a while, it became easier to just give in and go back to your old habit. This, incidentally, is why so many people who go on a diet, lose weight for a short time, then end up gaining it all back.

What happened? Why wasn't your willpower or conscious effort strong enough to change your long-term behavior—when that's what you really wanted?

What happened is that your brain is performing a process that neuroscientists are now calling *the Habit Loop.* The Habit Loop consists of three basic elements: the Cue, the Routine, and the Reward.

The first thing that causes a habit is called the *Cue.* This means that something happens in your world—a feeling, an emotion, a trigger—that tells your brain to go into automatic mode and start doing this particular habit.

Then there's the *Routine*. This can be a physical action, mental activity, or an emotional reaction. The Routine is the behavior that's triggered when the Cue occurs.

And then there is the *Reward*—a very literal prize that tells the brain that this particular habit is worth remembering and repeating.

For example, let's take the habit of drinking soda. You're going through your day and suddenly feel thirsty, tired, bored, or stressed. Any combination of these triggers may be present. So these stimuli become your Cue.

Now, let's take a step back and look inside the brain itself to see what's going on in there. Numerous scientific studies have shown that the human brain is a miracle of efficiency and organization. When we are first learning something new—any new habit, skill, or behavior—the brain uses a lot of energy to learn and master that new skill.

For example, remember when you first got your driver's license and had to back your car out of the garage for the very first time? If we could have peered into your brain at that moment, we would have seen a flurry of activity because this brand-new skill requires thousands of tiny complex calculations that must be performed in fractions of seconds to make sure you don't hit the gas too hard, don't hit the side of the garage, don't hit the garbage cans on the sidewalk, and don't hit any cars or pedestrians that may be coming down the street. That's a lot for any brain to handle!

But guess what? Now that you've fully mastered the skill of backing your car out of the garage, you literally *do not think about it.*

That means if we were to look at your brain on a brain scan machine today, we would see an incredible drop in brain activity when compared to the flood of activity that took place when you were first learning this new skill.

Which brings us back to today and the habit of drinking soda. First, there's the **Cue**—the trigger that happens in your environment the

THIS IS THE GOOD NEWS AND THE BAD NEWS ABOUT YOUR BRAIN.

first time you ever reached for a can of soda. In this instance, we might have seen a flurry of activity in your brain, just like we saw in the backing your car out of the garage example.

Today, however, just like driving, there is very little *conscious activity* in your brain when you reach for that soda. That's because your brain is highly efficient and conserves as much energy as possible in case it needs it for truly momentous things like fighting predators and raising children.

This very fact of the human brain is both the good news and the bad news about habits and their relationship to success. On the one hand, it's absolutely essential that you don't have to consciously think every time you perform simple activities every day like tying your shoes, brushing your teeth, or backing your car out of the garage.

However, because your brain is so efficient, it also makes it very hard to change a habit—even one you want to change—because your brain is saying in effect, "Hey, I've got a good thing going here. Why do you want to mess around with that?"

It's the classic "If it ain't broke, don't fix it!"

Yet this is happening inside your brain. That's what causes the second part of the Habit Loop called the **Routine**, the behavior you actually do once the Cue is triggered.

You feel stressed or thirsty—that's the Cue. You reach for the soda— that's the Routine. And the third step is the **Reward**: you feel more satiated and satisfied. Your brain essentially goes, *Thanks, I needed that.*

Yet here's the problem: the brain, at this level, cannot distinguish between a habit that is ultimately good for us and one that's ultimately bad for us.

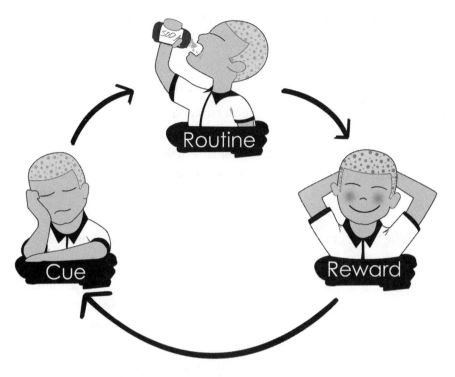

The Habit Loop

Good (productive) habits are the ones that move us toward our goal or destination, whether it's to be happy, healthy, lose weight, make more money, or finish our projects on time. Bad (unproductive) habits are the ones that stop us or prevent us from reaching our goal or destination. These are the habits that hold us back from the desired results we want and are perfectly capable of achieving.

WHY YOU HAVE SO MUCH SHELF-HELP

Can you now see that this very fact of human behavior is, in actuality, the essential problem in the personal growth industry?

The essential problem in the personal growth industry is that we have been told to change our behavior to get the things we want. And this makes perfect sense: after all, if we want to accomplish something new, doesn't it make sense that we have to change our behavior to get it?

HOW MUCH SHELF-HELP DO YOU HAVE?

Yet the problem is that our brains are wired to fight that very thing.

This is why I talk about the phenomenon I call **SHELF-Help**. *Shelf-help* means that millions of people are spending billions of dollars on behavior change books, seminars, coaching, and training. Yet the human brain—and last time I checked, most of the people investing in these programs are human beings—is wired to fight the very thing that all these programs are supposed to fix.

How, then, are we supposed to change our habits, when the very thing we're trying to change is fighting us every step of the way? And how is it possible that my coaching clients have achieved such incredible results—when the thing we're fighting is the very thing keeping us alive?

And how can we stop driving down the road of life with one foot on the brake, so we can finally, actually reach our goals?

That's what The Power Habits® System is all about.

STOP FIGHTING, START SUCCEEDING

If you want to create a more abundant lifestyle for yourself and your family, you will need to do something that's at once simpler than the old way, yet far more effective. And that is, to change your habits at the *subconscious* level and stop trying to use your *conscious willpower* to reach your goals.

That's because when you try to change your habits using your conscious mind or willpower, you are attempting to fight 95 percent of your brain (the subconscious mind) with 5 percent of your brain (the conscious mind). As you can now see, that is a strategy that is almost certain to fail.

What we really need is a proven SYSTEM that will empower you to do two things: first, bring your daily habits to your conscious awareness, so you can see what's holding you back from success in the first place; and second, systematically replace unproductive habits with productive habits (The Power Habits) so you can get your foot off the brake and reach your goals faster, easier, and with far less effort.

YOU'RE ABOUT TO LEARN A PROVEN SYSTEM SO YOU CAN DO THIS TOO.

Remember earlier when I talked about the four areas you can expect significant improvements in when you follow The Power Habits System? These key areas are **Relationships, Self-Confidence, Money,** and **Happiness.**

I want to point out that this System, because it's based on natural, fundamental principles of success, applies equally to individuals as well as couples, groups, teams, and organizations, large and small.

A *principle* is a fundamental law or truth that applies equally everywhere. For example, a principle in nature is gravity. If you jump out of an airplane, you're going to fall to the earth—no matter how positive or negative, rich or poor, happy or unhappy you are. The principle of gravity affects everyone equally, no matter what the situation.

Just like gravity, the principles I share in this book and in my training programs apply equally to individuals, departments, teams, companies, and organizations, regardless of size. They also apply to marriages, intimate relationships, families, and groups of two or more people involved in any kind of personal or professional relationship.

As the founder of SuccessClinic.com, I'm honored to lead what has become one of the world's leading global success training companies. People and organizations in over 120 countries are now using my methods to reach their goals with less time, money, and effort and manifest their desires like clockwork. I'm also privileged to have the world's top thought leaders in business and personal growth endorse my programs.

Yet things didn't start out this way. Let me explain...

MY STORY (IN BRIEF)

Even though it's a total cliché, I grew up poor in a rich neighborhood. Before I was three years old, my father moved my family from New Jersey to Kennebunkport, Maine, one of the wealthiest communities in New England. Yet my family was dirt poor.

And I mean that literally, because we lived at the bottom of a dirt road in a drafty, unfinished house. One day when I was about nine years old, I asked my mother, "Mom, how come you and Dad are always fighting about money?"

My mother replied that they constantly fought about money because there wasn't enough money coming in and she was afraid they wouldn't be able to pay the bills and keep food on the table.

When she said that, I was very confused, because I saw both my parents working hard all the time. Weeks would go by and we would hardly see my father because he'd be working 70 or 80 hours a week. And my mother worked part-time jobs too.

So I asked her the next question that popped into my head: "Why isn't there enough money?"

I don't think my mother really knew how to answer that question, so she took out the family checkbook and showed me how much money was coming in and going out every month. And sure enough, there was more MONTH left at the end of the MONEY!

At that moment, I made two decisions: First, I decided that I wouldn't ask my parents for anything. Now I'm sure that was not my mother's intention. Nevertheless, I decided not to ask for things, because I didn't want to be a burden to my family. The second decision I made was that I was going to make something of my life—even though I had no idea what that meant, let alone how to do it.

But I realized that I hated that life of lack and fear and poverty and not-enoughness. And I also came to realize that life didn't have to be that way—because right down the street, I saw people who had things like money, nice clothes, and food (there was never enough food in our house).

You've heard of the book *Rich Dad Poor Dad*? Well, I only had a "poor dad." My father, even though he worked hard all his life, couldn't teach me how to be successful. Not because he didn't want to, but because he simply didn't have the skills or knowledge to do it himself. And since I decided that I wanted a different life—one that didn't include poverty and not-enoughness—and since I didn't know whom to ask or what else to do, I decided to go to the library.

I began devouring the classics of self-help literature: Dale Carnegie, Napoleon Hill, Stephen Covey, and more. I spent most of my childhood in the library reading self-help books because I believed those books could help me escape from that life of poverty.

EVERYONE TOLD ME I WAS GOING TO BE A BIG SUCCESS.

I also worked hard in school because I assumed that the best way to get ahead in life was to get good grades—since that's what every adult told me. So, I got straight A's, skipped eighth grade, graduated at the top of my class, and got full scholarships to college.

By the time I graduated from high school, my parents, teachers, and friends were telling me that I was going to be a big success. Unfortunately, they were all wrong.

I went to college for one year and then decided to leave college to pursue my dream of becoming a professional ballet dancer. After a career-ending injury at age 21, I became the most over-educated underachiever you ever saw.

I found myself in a series of "survival jobs," and I hated each one more than the last. Then one night in October 1997, quite by accident, I finally discovered the secret, the answer that changed my life.

In fact, when I made this discovery, not only did it explain my entire life up to that point; more importantly, my discovery has given countless thousands of people around the world the answers in their search for success.

And I was shocked to see that NOT ONE of the "gurus" to whom I had given so much of my time, energy, and money had ever mentioned it. But I'm getting ahead of myself…

WHY I'M SHARING THESE SECRETS

As I mentioned earlier, I've been blessed to help countless thousands of people just like you to achieve more wealth, success, and happiness using my Power Habits® System. Yet what I didn't tell you was that it's for a much larger purpose.

You see, I started SuccessClinic.com in 1997 with nothing but $800 to my name and a book on how to do HTML. Yet I did have one other thing—a dream. I had a dream, a mission, and a vision to create a system that *anyone* could use to become highly successful and to launch a company that would help raise the consciousness of the Earth.

My greatest mission now is to train coaches who can duplicate what I've done with my clients and empower more people around the world with the tools to financial freedom and fulfillment.

Whether you want to hit your first $10K in your business, or you're working to get to $100K a year, or you're ready to make your first (or your next) million and beyond, my greatest happiness comes when I get to coach and mentor hardworking, impact-driven people like you to become the next greatest version of themselves.

However, this means that aside from a select group of entrepreneurs, business professionals, and mastermind students, many people may never get the chance to work with me personally. That's why I'm honored to publish this book, because it's my mission to get this material into the hands of as many people as possible around the world, so that even more people can benefit from this teaching.

Now, remember all those traditional success programs you've tried before? They taught you how to succeed, and that's a good thing, right?

I mean, if you want to do something, you need to know how to do it, don't you? And since we all want to succeed, then all we need is to be told how to succeed and then we'd all be very successful, right?

In the next chapter, I'll show you why that single assumption is costing you a fortune right now, and I'll also reveal the life-changing discovery I made one fateful night in 1997 that led to the creation of The Power Habits® System...

CHAPTER 5

SUCCESS ANOREXIA—A SIMPLE DISCOVERY THAT CHANGED THE UNIVERSE

"There is no influence like the influence of habit."
— Gilbert Parker

On the evening of October 20, 1997, I accidentally made a discovery that changed my life—and the lives of countless thousands of people just like you around the world.

On that fateful night, I found myself attending a seminar on eating disorders. Remember how I told you that I had a (very short) career as a professional ballet dancer? In that profession, sadly, it's very common for people to develop eating disorders like anorexia and bulimia. And since so many of my friends and colleagues over the years had developed eating disorders, I decided to attend the seminar to learn more about it.

It's important to note that I had never developed an eating disorder. As you may recall, growing up, food was scarce in my household. So I developed a love of food—that is, whenever I could get it!

At the time of the seminar, I was a religious studies major in college. After listening to *The 7 Habits of Highly Effective People* over and over again on audiotape, I decided to follow in Dr. Stephen Covey's footsteps because of the profound effect that his book had on me. I discovered that Dr. Covey had done his undergraduate work in the field of religious studies, so I decided to do the same thing.

At the seminar that evening, the speaker described why so many smart, creative, talented, sensitive people—mostly young women—develop eating disorders. She said that it was not a matter of nutrition or of needing to teach these women which foods to eat.

After a great deal of research and study, the speaker concluded that the person suffering from an eating disorder was acting from a desire not to be here on Earth. In essence, *she was punishing herself because of a deeply negative self-image.*

As the speaker described the type of person who develop eating disorders, I noticed something I never expected to happen: *I realized that she was describing me to a T.*

She said that people who starve themselves tend to be smart, creative, and talented. *Check.*

They're usually straight-A students and overachievers in school. *Check.*

They're also hypersensitive individuals who put other people's needs ahead of their own. *Check, check, and double-check.*

The speaker then said the sentence that changed the universe…

She said that these individuals almost never eat—but when they do eat, they settle for crumbs.

THAT WAS THE MOMENT MY LIFE MADE SENSE FOR THE FIRST TIME.

While I knew that this description didn't fit me in relation to food—because I've always enjoyed food—in that moment, I had a startling realization:

*Wait a minute. I haven't been settling for crumbs of food. I've been settling for **the crumbs of LIFE!***

It was at that moment that my life made sense for the very first time.

ARE YOU STARVING YOURSELF OF SUCCESS?

When we talk about eating disorders such as *anorexia* or *bulimia*, we're typically talking about habits that relate to the starvation or bingeing and purging of food.

For example, *anorexia* is defined as "an emotional disorder characterized by an obsessive desire to lose weight by refusing to eat"; while *bulimia* is defined as "an emotional disorder involving distortion of body image and an obsessive desire to lose weight, in which bouts of extreme overeating are followed by depression and self-induced vomiting, purging, or fasting."

On that fateful night at the seminar, I became aware that I was *settling for the crumbs of life.* And at that moment, I realized that just like millions of people are starving themselves of food, we humans could also *starve ourselves of success.*

For example, since the beginning of time, women have been taught that their worth comes from their physical bodies. Make no mistake about it—a woman's worth does not come from her physical body! Yet for centuries, female human beings have been *told* or *taught* that their worth is based on their appearance or their physical bodies.

So, let's say you have a human being who's been taught that her worth comes from her physical body (even though it's not true, it's what she's been told). Let's further assume that this person develops a very low sense of self-worth—what I call a person's **head trash**—and begins to subconsciously punish herself. So you take a person who's been taught that her worth comes from her physical body…add to that a very low sense of self-worth…

Doesn't it make sense that this person will punish that part of herself that she was told her worth comes from—namely, her physical body? And if you're going to punish your physical body, isn't *starving yourself of food* a great way to do it?

I realize that very few female human beings were literally told that "your worth comes from your physical body." Yet if you happen to live on planet Earth and are female, it's nearly impossible for this belief not to have affected you, simply because it's been perpetuated for so long and by so many.

Which brings us to the other sex—namely, men. If women have been taught that their worth comes from their physical bodies, where have men been taught their worth comes from?

I've asked that question hundreds of times in front of tens of thousands of people at my keynote speeches, private workshops, and live events. And the universal answer is always the same: men, since the beginning of time, have been taught their worth comes from their possessions, their title, their job, their level of success, their net worth, their holdings, where they live, what kind of car they drive, the amount of money in their bank accounts—in short, what I call their *material bodies* (to distinguish it from their *physical bodies*).

Of course, a man's worth does not come from his material body, any more than a woman's worth comes from her physical body. Nevertheless, men have been taught that their worth comes from their material bodies since the beginning of human history.

> **IF YOU WANT TO PUNISH YOUR PHYSICAL BODY, IT MAKES SENSE TO STARVE YOURSELF OF FOOD.**

> IF YOU WANT TO PUNISH YOUR MATERIAL BODY, IT MAKES SENSE TO STARVE YOURSELF OF SUCCESS.

So now let's say you have a human being who has been taught that his worth comes from his material body (even though it's not true, it's what he's been told). Now let's assume that this person develops a very low sense of self-worth—their *head trash*—and begins to subconsciously punish himself. So you take a person who's been taught that his worth comes from his material body...add to that a very low sense of self-worth...

Doesn't it make sense that he will punish that part of himself that he was told his worth comes from—namely, his material body? And if you're going to punish your material body, wouldn't developing the habit of *starving yourself of success* be a great way to do it?

SUCCESS ANOREXIA AND POWER HABITS

At 8:20 P.M. on October 20, 1997, I became the first person to realize the existence of a condition that I named **success anorexia**. Just like *anorexia* is "an emotional disorder characterized by refusing to eat," *success anorexia* is defined as "an emotional disorder characterized by self-sabotage or refusing to succeed."

Yes, I know this sounds crazy. However, as a result of my "accidental" discovery, I also realized that millions of people around the world had unknowingly and unwittingly developed the habit of starving themselves of success—yet had no idea why this was happening or how to fix the problem.

That's when I knew I had to get this information out to the millions of people just like me—people who were unconsciously stopping themselves from the success they were perfectly capable of achieving.

And that's when The Power Habits® System was born.

PHYSICAL AND MATERIAL BODY PRESSURES

You may have noticed that while the people who starve themselves of food tend to be women, the people who starve themselves of success tend to be men. But what if you're a woman who's starving yourself of success? How is that possible?

Over the last 50 years, women have entered the workforce in unprecedented numbers. In fact, statistics show that not only do women outnumber men in the American workforce, women are also starting new businesses at a higher rate than men.

This means that in addition to being told that their worth comes from their physical bodies, women are now ALSO being told that their worth comes from their material bodies. For example, many women today are facing the dual pressures of having to look perfect in addition to "bringing home the bacon."

Which means that women today are often facing *material body pressure* in addition to *physical body pressure.* Oh, joy!

Although few are consciously aware of it, many women are starving themselves of both food and success. In fact, many of my female clients came to me initially because they were holding themselves back from success, yet later told me that at one time in their lives they were anorexic or bulimic.

> **MILLIONS OF WOMEN TODAY ARE STARVING THEMSELVES OF FOOD AND SUCCESS.**

After working with thousands of people in my coaching practice, live seminars, and mastermind programs, I've come to realize that we human beings have two great fears: the fear of expressing Who We Really Are, and the fear of NOT expressing Who We Really Are.

My friend Neale Donald Walsch, author of the *Conversations with God* series, puts it like this: "Since the beginning of time, all we've ever wanted is to love and be loved. And since the beginning of time, all we have stopped from happening is to love and be loved." That's why one of the goals of this program is to give you permission to express Who You Really Are—*Permission to Succeed®*.[1]

THE NATURALS OF SUCCESS

There's a select group of people you often see on TV, in the movies, or on stage winning award after award every year at your company's annual sales convention. They're the people I call **the Naturals of Success**.

You've heard of *the 80/20 Rule*, also known as "Pareto's Principle"— which states that 80 percent of your results come from 20 percent of your efforts. Yet in today's society, what seems to be more accurate is *the 98/2 Rule*—because the vast majority of the world's wealth (about 98 percent) is held by just 2 percent of the population.

While it doesn't seem fair, the majority of the money, success, and wealth in the world is held by a tiny minority of people. There's just one problem: these highly successful people usually can't tell you how they got there. And why is that? Because the Naturals are *unconsciously competent at allowing themselves to succeed.*

Okay, I know that was a mouthful—so let's unpack that sentence...

---

1   *Permission to Succeed®* is the title of my first book that was first published by my company SuccessClinic.com in 1998 and subsequently published by the *Chicken Soup for the Soul* publisher in 1999.

THE FOUR STAGES OF COMPETENCE

Whenever you're learning something new or mastering a new skill or habit—for example, tying your shoe, driving a car, making a million dollars—you invariably go through *the four stages of competence.*

Stage 1 is *unconscious incompetence*, which means you don't know that you don't know.

Stage 2 is *conscious incompetence*, which means you know that you don't know.

Stage 3 is *conscious competence*, which means you know that you know.

Stage 4 is *unconscious competence*, which means you do it without conscious thought.

For example, think about driving a car. Remember the first time you were in a car when you were an infant? Probably not. You probably weren't thinking, "Gee, when I grow up, I want to drive this...what are these things called again?"

The point is you are driven around by someone else (unless your parents let you drive when you were an infant, in which case we really need to talk), and the thought of driving a car never entered your mind. At this stage, you were *unconsciously incompetent* because you didn't know that you didn't know.

Then, when you got a little older, you began to think, "Hey, these goofy adults have these weird things called *cars*, and all I have is a bicycle, which I can't get very far with. I definitely want to get away from my parents, but I don't know how to drive a car yet. I think I want to learn how to drive a car."

> **THE NATURALS ARE UNCONSCIOUSLY COMPETENT AT ALLOWING THEMSELVES TO SUCCEED.**

Now you're at the stage of *conscious incompetence*, because you know that you don't know.

Then, when you got a little older still, you finally took driver's ed, learned how to drive a car, and got your driver's license. You were then at the stage of *conscious competence,* because you knew that you knew (and could prove it; hence the license to drive).

And today, when you're driving your car, you're talking on the phone (hands-free and not texting, right?), sipping your coffee, switching between radio stations, thinking about your next meeting, getting one kid to stop torturing the other—"So help me, I'll pull this car over!"—and, oh yeah, driving. You are now *unconsciously competent* at driving a car, because you are performing this skill or habit *without conscious thought.*

THE NATURALS DON'T HAVE HEAD TRASH ABOUT SUCCESS.

In fact, today you are unconsciously competent at dozens, perhaps hundreds of skills or habits that you do every day—for example, tying your shoes, brushing your teeth, getting dressed, getting undressed, eating, drinking, speaking, reading, writing, typing, using your remote control (no, the other one), checking your email, checking your voicemail, checking your social media accounts, and so on.

Let's go back to the Naturals of Success, those lucky few who have what the rest of the world wants. The counterintuitive secret about the Naturals is that they are **unconsciously competent at allowing themselves to succeed**. What does that mean? It means that while the rest of the world is striving, trying, struggling, toiling, and straining to achieve success, the Naturals are nonchalantly accumulating success—because they don't have the **head trash** that's holding the rest of us back.

As if that weren't bad enough, there's another problem with the Naturals—because when you are unconsciously competent at doing something, you often don't know or can't explain how you are doing that thing. This explains why so many people have spent tens of thousands of dollars (or more) on traditional "success" programs, yet still haven't achieved the success they desire—because those programs are usually taught by the Naturals.

WHAT HITTING A GOLF BALL TAUGHT ME ABOUT SUCCESS

For example, I enjoy playing golf (even though I suck at it, I still enjoy it). One day, I decided that I wanted to improve my golf game—you know, to actually hit the ball in the air once in a while. So I went to the practice tee to work on my swing.

As I was hacking away without much success, I saw another golfer hitting the ball a mile time after time off the tee. So I went up to him and asked him his secret. He replied, "Just grip it and rip it."

Wow, thanks—that was really helpful!

Of course, this man didn't owe me an explanation or coaching—after all, I hadn't paid him for his advice. Yet how many times HAVE you paid someone for their advice—a "guru" or so-called "expert"—and they essentially gave you an answer equivalent to "just grip it and rip it?"

For example, when I launched SuccessClinic.com in 1997 in my college dorm room with $800 to my name, I knew that I didn't know how to run a successful online business. In other words, I was *consciously incompetent* at running a business, because I knew that I didn't know what to do or how to do it. I decided to take action to fix that, because I had a dream to help people and make a difference in the lives of millions of people around the globe.

So I ended up hiring a bunch of "gurus" and paid them (collectively) more than $500,000 to teach me how to build my business. Now I didn't have half a million dollars sitting around my dorm room; as I shared with you, I had less than $800 to my name when I started.

However, I remembered a quote from Benjamin Franklin: "If a man empties his purse into his head, no man can take it away from him. An investment in knowledge always pays the best interest."

> I PAID THE "GURUS" MORE THAN $500,000.00 AND GOT NOTHING TO SHOW FOR IT.

So I decided to "empty my purse into my head"—meaning, as soon as money would come into the business, I would immediately invest it in my own education so I could help more people.

Unfortunately, there was one big problem: even after paying them thousands of dollars, most of these self-proclaimed "gurus" were such sucky teachers or so unconsciously competent at success that they ended up taking my money *and* sapping my self-confidence at the same time.

Have you had something like that happen to you too? Well, I'm here to tell you that **it's not your fault**.

Going back to my golf example, once I realized that I couldn't get very far on my own or with free advice, I decided to hire a golf coach. Now this coach couldn't hit the ball as far as the guy I saw on the tee, yet he was a far better teacher.

That's because he patiently broke down each step of my golf swing and explained how changing just a few small things would make a big difference. For example, in one of our lessons, he said that I needed to open the clubface when I struck the ball.

I said, "What's a clubface?"

He replied, "That would be the face of the club. Club. Face."

"Oh," I said.

At the end of just two lessons, I was hitting the ball farther than I had ever hit it before. That's when I realized two things: First, it sure is fun to finally get RESULTS when you invest in yourself!

Second, I realized that the true causes of success are often hidden and counterintuitive, especially to those people who are *unconsciously competent* at it.

That's why it took someone like me—the nerdiest nerd in the business and personal growth industry—to break down **The Power Habits® of Unconsciously Successful People** and systemize them, so anybody can do it!

CRAVING, ANYONE?

I want you to understand something absolutely key here: self-sabotaging behaviors that hold you back from success are precisely that— behaviors. A *behavior* is something you do that is caused by something else. You do not do anything without a reason.

For example, why do you bathe every day before going to work? Because you probably wouldn't like the way you felt (or smelled) if you *didn't* do it. Bathing before work is one of the many unconscious habits you do every day without thinking about it.

However, let me ask you a question: Could you, if you wanted to, NOT bathe before going into work? Of course you could. So, why do you continue do it?

You bathe before work because it's a habit you're used to and because you wouldn't like the results if you *didn't* do it. Remember the Habit Loop we looked at in the last chapter? Well, this is where we add the next component of the Habit Loop.

Recall that the Habit Loop consists of the three parts I mentioned earlier: the Cue, or environmental trigger; the Routine, or habitual

THE HABIT LOOP CAUSES CRAVING.

behavior; and the Reward, which is the good feeling your brain receives after performing the Routine.

Yet there is another, even more subtle element of the Habit Loop that is known by the very scientific term called *Craving*.

For example, let's go back to our drinking soda example. Now you know that you desire to lose weight: that's your goal. Furthermore, you know that you should drink more water and less soda in order to reach your goal. That's your *conscious awareness* of what you should do to reach your goal.

However, in this example, you've developed the habit of drinking soda throughout the day. So, your Habit Loop looks like this:

Cue = feeling thirsty, tired, bored, or stressed

Routine = drink soda

Reward = your brain feels satisfied

But guess what? There's something else going on here in the brain. That something else is called *Craving*.

For instance, have you ever found yourself wandering by a plate of chocolate chip cookies and felt *irresistibly drawn* to take one? Even if you weren't really hungry, you probably felt the compulsion to take one anyway. Why?

The answer is because somewhere in your brain is the imprint of all those yummy chocolate chip cookies you've ever eaten (and for some of us, that's a pretty big memory bank). Remember how we looked at how efficient your brain is? According to scientific research, your brain stores countless millions of memories or sensations that enable you to make faster, better decisions about what to do and what not to do thousands of times every day.

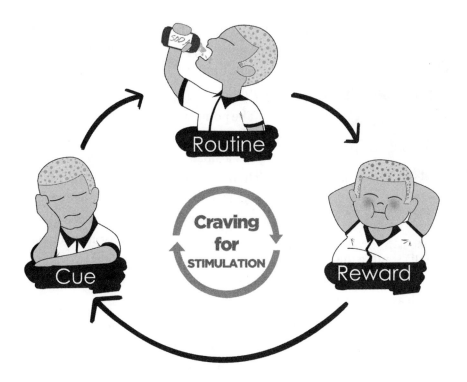

The Habit Loop Causes Craving

For example, somewhere in your brain is the knowledge that you should not eat a shoe and that chocolate chip cookies taste pretty good. I know it sounds silly, but think about how hard our daily lives would be if our brains didn't do this. We might go around chewing on tables and chairs and couches and shoes if our brains didn't store this helpful information.

The point is, if your brain has a prior sensation of how good a chocolate chip cookie tastes, your brain has encoded what's called a *craving* for chocolate chip cookies. In fact, as you've been reading about these yummy chocolate chip cookies for the last minute or so, I'll bet

93

COMPANIES SPEND MILLIONS EACH YEAR TO KEEP YOUR BRAIN ADDICTED TO THEIR PRODUCTS.

you're thinking, "Dang, a chocolate chip cookie sounds good right about now!" (I'm thinking the same thing as I'm writing these sentences to you!)

The point is, for some of us, it's the same with that can of soda. Inside your brain, there's a small area called the *basal ganglia*, which neuroscientists have pinpointed as the area that controls many of our daily habits. For example, if you've had a few cans of soda in your lifetime and enjoy the taste of it, your basal ganglia sends a message to the rest of your brain around three o'clock in the afternoon that says: "Hey, make sure we get more of this stuff in our mouth as soon as possible!"

And guess what? Soft drink companies spend untold millions of dollars each year trying to figure out exactly what causes these cravings in the human brain and add chemicals and sweeteners to ensure that once you have that first taste of their soda pop, you're going to want more and more and more of it.

You will develop a literal *craving* for it, such that if you go too long without it, you'll actually feel like you're being deprived. This is precisely why these kinds of habits are so hard to break—because it's not just the Cue, the Routine, and the Reward we're dealing with. We're also dealing with the Craving that happens *in the brain*—even when we're not actually performing the habit!

This Craving, or desire to get a Reward from performing a particular habit, explains why so many people who really want to quit smoking can't do it, no matter how hard they try. It also explains why it's so hard to stick to a diet, even if you really want to lose weight. It also explains why compulsive gamblers keep gambling, even when they've lost their home, their family, and their dignity—because the smoker craves the nicotine, the dieter craves the sweets, and the gambler craves the emotional rush that comes from gambling. And in each of their brains is *the literal sensation of deprivation* if that Craving is not fulfilled.

WHY WE PROCRASTINATE

But how does this explain a common habit like *procrastination?* Everyone knows that "procrastination is the thief of time." We all realize that procrastination is an unproductive (many would say bad) habit that costs us not just time, but also money and opportunity.

As I've said to countless thousands of people in my keynote speeches, private workshops, and live seminars around the world, is there anyone who would argue that procrastination is a good habit that helps us reach our goals? Of course not! Why, then, do so many hardworking, mission-driven people—people who really want to make a difference and reach their goals—keep doing this costly habit that they know they shouldn't do? And what could we possibly *crave* when it comes to doing something so obviously against our own best interests?

Let's look at a common example of someone who procrastinates and examine why it happens. Let's say the **Cue** in this example is having a deadline to complete a project—something like, oh I don't know, writing a book and making sure you send the manuscript to your publisher by a certain date (ahem).

So your Cue in this example is you're thinking about doing that thing you know you should be doing.

What's the **Routine** in this example? The Routine is putting it off until the last possible minute—and *doing something else* to fill up the time. In the illustration below,

THIS IS WHY WE DO THINGS THAT WE KNOW AREN'T GOOD FOR US.

I asked my graphic designer to put in the Routine an image of someone watching cat videos on YouTube.

And what's better than watching cat videos on YouTube? Exactly—nothing!

So what's the **Reward** we get from NOT doing the thing we know we should do—the thing we know will help us advance our career (like finishing a book would) or help us reach our goals?

This is where it gets interesting. Remember, we are talking about the Reward in the brain—that miraculous organ whose #1 job is to keep us not-dead. In other words, your brain—the lizard brain, basal ganglia, or survival brain—has one primary function, and that is to make sure you don't die.

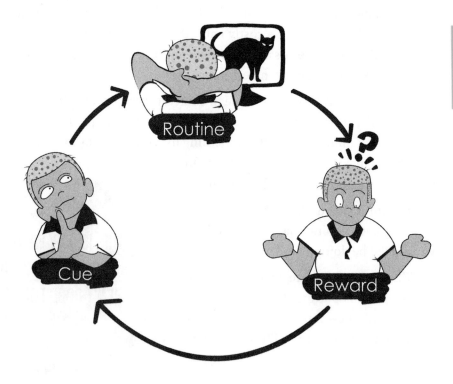

And what's one great way to make sure you don't die? To keep you from anything that causes fear!

For example, when you're thinking about doing that thing that could advance your career, there's one other thing that could happen—and that is, it could NOT advance your career.

When you're thinking about writing that article, calling that prospect, filming that video, or finishing that online course you bought, the problem is that your brain is smart enough to know that, just as easily as it could help you reach your goals, it could also NOT help you reach your goals.

Which is why, as counterintuitive as it sounds, the Reward in the brain for procrastinating is *the feeling of SAFETY.*

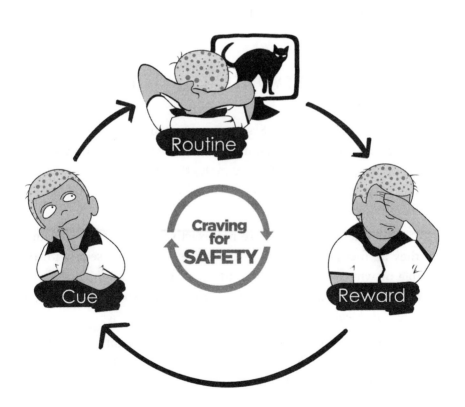

Because your lizard brain's main function is to keep you not-dead, when you face the prospect of something that scares you—an instance where you could "fail"—your brain essentially goes into "fight, flight, or freeze" mode.

And what's the best way not to fail? To not take any action in the first place!

What would be the **Craving** in this case? If the Reward is the feeling of safety, the Craving in the brain would be *the Craving for safety.*

Your brain craves safety because to your brain, safety means, "I'm not going to do this, which means I'm not going to die today." Which means, as strange as it sounds, the habit of procrastination is actually caused by your brain's desire not to die.

Can you now see why trying to use "willpower" to fight the habit of procrastination is an exercise in futility?

ON BEYOND BEHAVIOR

Before my Power Habits® System, most attempts to fix the age-old question of "how to stop sabotaging yourself" were focused on trying to change a person's behavior. For example, the "gurus" told us to "think positive, set your goals, just do it"—all of which make sense and none of which are inherently wrong.

Yet while these commands are not exactly "wrong," the problem is that they all focus on *conscious behaviors.* As you've just seen with the example of why we procrastinate, the confusing and annoying fact is that *it's very difficult to change a habitual pattern of behavior by focusing on changing your behavior.*

Therefore, we must go beneath the behavior (or habit) to *the hidden reasons why we do the behavior in the first place.* As I've said to countless audiences and coaching clients around the globe for more than two decades, if we want to empower ourselves to make real, lasting change, we must go beneath the symptom level to the causal level.

THIS IS WHAT MAKES MY POWER HABITS® SYSTEM SO POWERFUL AND EFFECTIVE.

That's what makes my Power Habits System so different—and so stunningly effective. Because when you follow the System, you'll no longer be trying to change your life by focusing on symptoms or behaviors; you're going to go beyond behavior to what causes it in the first place.

That's one of the main reasons why my clients experience such dramatic, life-changing results—because even if you've already spent tens of thousands (or more) on traditional "success" programs with little to show for it, once you start following my Power Habits System, the results can come faster than you ever imagined.

What's even more exciting about following The Power Habits System is that *you cannot hold yourself back from success* if you learn and adopt these new Power Habits. That's because when you follow my Power Habits System, you will be eliminating the causes of self-sabotage and "foot-on-the-brake syndrome" at the causal (or subconscious) level.

I'm not saying this to make you feel good; I'm saying this because it's based on my firsthand experience working with countless thousands of men, women, and children from all walks of life around the world since 1997.

THE POWER HABITS® OF UNCONSCIOUSLY SUCCESSFUL PEOPLE

Now that you know the benefits you'll get when you follow my System and what you need to do to get those benefits, it's time to reveal The 11 Power Habits® of Unconsciously Successful People.

These 11 Power Habits are simple to understand, yet require conscious effort to do. Beginning with Power Habit #1, you will begin to replace your unproductive habits with productive Power Habits every step of the way, so you can stop stopping yourself from success and start enjoying the success, happiness, and fulfillment you desire and are capable of achieving.

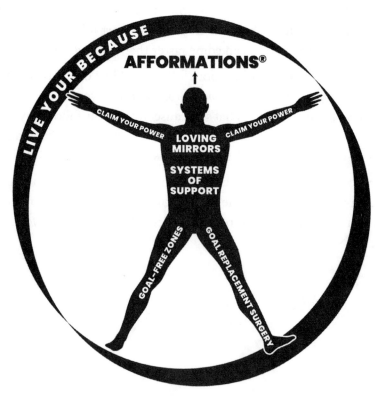

THE POWER HABITS® FRAMEWORK

Power Habit #1 is **Use AFFORMATIONS®**. No, I didn't spell that word wrong. *Afformations®* are empowering questions, not statements, that immediately change your subconscious thought patterns from negative to positive. Using Afformations will enable you to reprogram your subconscious thought patterns, attract more abundance, and manifest your desires faster and easier than ever before.

In **Power Habit #2, Engage Your Loving Mirrors**, you'll learn how to gain unconditional support for your life, career, and relationships. This is one of the foundational Power Habits that highly successful people always do, and it's essential that you do it too.

If you want to reach your full potential, **Power Habits #3 through #7** are to **Install Your Systems of Support.** Just like your house and your body, your life and your business have essential systems that must function properly to create maximum success with minimum effort. In these habits, you'll learn what these systems are and how to install them in your life and your business.

Power Habits #8 and #9 deal with the question of where and how your goals fit into your life. In **Power Habit #8**, you'll **Practice Goal-Free Zones** and discover why it's so important to re-energize and revitalize yourself on a consistent, daily basis. In **Power Habit #9, Perform Goal Replacement Surgery**, you'll discover if your stated goals are really yours—or if they are someone else's that you've internalized.

Power Habit #10 is called **Claim Your Power**. Many people have abandoned their own inner power due to environmental factors or external pressures. That means that instead of pursuing their own dreams, they've developed the habit of setting aside their true desires. That's why this habit involves doing simple yet powerful strategies so that you make your dreams just as important as anyone else's.

Finally, **Power Habit #11, Live Your Because**, deals with your mission, your purpose on Earth, your Ultimate Why-To. Most people don't know why they're here on Earth, and this can lead to feelings ranging from frustration, anger, and stress, all the way to depression and the depths of despair. When you Live Your Because and make The Power Habits System a part of your everyday life, you will not only know why you're here on Earth; you will finally have the tools to create a more abundant lifestyle for yourself, your family, and the world.

So, dear reader... Are you ready to get your foot off the brake and finally live the life you've imagined?

NOAH'S NOTES (IN A NUTSHELL)

1. Most people want to improve one or more areas of their lives—health, wealth, business, relationships, etc.—and have spent a lot of time, money, and effort to do that.

2. Yet millions of people remain frustrated, overwhelmed, or just stuck, because what they were told to do was either incomplete or just plain wrong.

3. **The Naturals of Success** are *unconsciously competent at allowing themselves to succeed.* That means two things: they often don't know what they're doing that's causing their success and they usually can't teach what they're doing either.

4. That's one of the main reasons that millions of people who've really tried to achieve success haven't gotten the results they wanted: because they were going to the wrong people for advice, coaching, or training.

5. Your results in life are determined by two things: the quality of your communication with the world *inside* you and the

quality of your communication with the world *outside* you. These are called **your Inner Game** and **Outer Game**, respectively.

6. When you only focus on Inner Game or Outer Game, it's going to be very difficult, if not impossible, for you to enjoy long-term, lasting success.

7. Moreover, based on more than two decades of research and experience, 90 percent of your success comes from Inner Game Mastery, while only 10 percent comes from Outer Game Systems.

8. I teach **The Power Habits® of Unconsciously Successful People**, and the primary reason for my coaching clients collectively adding **more than $2.2 billion in sales** is because they followed my Power Habits® System—a proven, step-by-step formula for Inner Game Mastery and Outer Game Systems, that cannot be taught by the Naturals of Success.

PART 2

THE POWER HABITS® SYSTEM

CHAPTER 6

POWER HABIT #1: USE AFFORMATIONS®

"Every sentence I utter must be understood not as an affirmation, but as a question."
— Niels Bohr

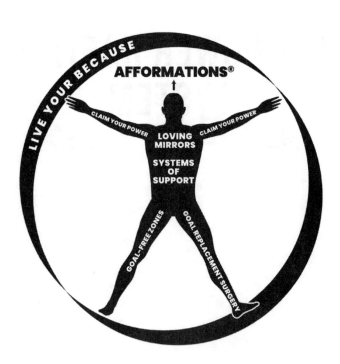

D id you ever notice how the best ideas come to you in the shower?

It happens all the time. You're minding your own business, holding the shampoo bottle, when suddenly it hits you—the idea that would change everything, the solution to the problem you've been facing, the answer to the question you've been asking…and it was right in front of you all along.

THE SHOWER THAT CHANGED EVERYTHING

April 24, 1997: a crisp spring morning in New England. I'm living in a dorm room at the small liberal arts college where I'm majoring in religious studies. The dorm room itself is sizable enough that simply by standing in the middle of the room, you could touch the walls on either side.

At this point in my life, I'm 30 years old, divorced, and have less than $800 to my name. I also have no idea what I'm going to do with the rest of my life.

On the night before, I'm sitting in this tiny room, staring at the concrete walls, when three thoughts occur to me. The first thought is that something is hugely wrong with my life, and that much is obvious.

The second thought, which bothers me even more than the first, is that I have no idea how to fix my life. That one definitely bugs me.

The third thought, which bothers me even more than the first two, is that if anyone should be successful, it's me. And since I'm anything but successful, I definitely feel like a complete and utter failure.

For as long as I could remember, I'd had this inescapable nagging feeling that there was something missing, some vital piece of information I'd overlooked, some secret key that would unlock the vault to success. But the more I looked, the harder I tried, the more the answers seemed to elude me. That was the night before The Shower That Changed Everything.

Something else happens that's important to our story. As I'm sitting in my miniature dorm room thinking about how my life pretty much sucks, I look around the room and see something. In fact, I see lots of somethings.

I realize that the walls of my dorm room are covered with pieces of yellow legal paper on which I had written dozens of positive statements—statements like "I'm happy," "I am rich," and "I'm good enough."

Why had I posted all these positive statements all over my room? Because that's what all those self-help books I've been reading for so many years told me to do!

I finally admit something that I never wanted to admit before: that even though I had spent most of my life trying to convince myself of the truth of these statements, I never really believed them.

As much as I wanted to believe that I was happy, rich, and good enough, I didn't believe any of those things. And the harder I tried to believe those positive things about my life, the more the cold hard facts stared back at me and seemed to say, "Who are you kidding?" I turn out the light and go to bed feeling depressed, defeated, and discouraged.

The next day, I get up and get in the shower just like any other morning, except on this particular morning, my mind is still racing from the night before. Questions start bouncing around my head—questions that are simple yet profound.

If you could have heard what was going on in my head at that exact moment, it would have sounded like this:

If I've been saying these positive statements to myself for so many years, how come I don't believe them?

If I don't believe these positive statements after repeating them over and over again for so long, what's it going to take for me to finally believe something good about myself?

There's got to be an easier way to change my life, but what is it?

That's when it hit me. (No, not the soap.)

I realize that what I'm doing at that very moment is asking and searching for answers to questions. In that instant, I realize that *human thought itself is the process of asking and searching for answers to questions.*

Suddenly, a question forms itself in my mind—a simple question that changed everything...

I DID IT BECAUSE THAT'S WHAT ALL THOSE "GURUS" TOLD ME TO DO!

"If human thought is the process of asking and searching for answers to questions, why are we making statements that we don't believe?"

Suddenly, I finally understand why I never believed all those positive statements I'd been saying all those years. It all came down to one simple thing. Of course it was so obvious now, but I realized that no matter how long or how often I repeated those positive statements to myself, if I didn't fix this one thing, all of my efforts would be for nothing.

Then something else occurs to me: I realize there are millions of people just like me—people who are trying really hard to change their lives, who are following the rules just like we were told, but who still haven't manifested the lifestyle they really want—because they don't believe the positive statements they've been saying to themselves either.

At that moment, I have the realization that if we *start to ask ourselves the right questions* and *stop asking the wrong questions,* it would change everything. And for the first time in my life, I know in the depths of my soul what I'm here on Earth to do.

HOW YOU'VE BEEN TOLD
TO CHANGE YOUR LIFE

We've already examined many of the methods people have tried to change their lives. These include:

✓ Reading self-help books

✓ Buying personal growth programs

✓ Attending conferences and seminars

✓ Writing your goals

✓ Doing vision boards

✓ Using affirmations

Wait a minute. What's that last one?

If you've ever read a self-help book or tried anything in our industry, it's very likely you've tried using affirmations to change your life. Why? Because that's what every "traditional success teacher" tells you to do.

Do "affirmations" actually work to change our lives? Of course they do. Affirmations have helped millions of people achieve their personal and professional goals.

However, there's just one teeny little problem…

What is an affirmation? Simply put, an *affirmation* is a statement of something you want to be true in your life.

Your thoughts are like seeds; you plant these **thought-seeds** every minute of every hour of every day, whether you're aware of it or not.

As you think about anything—life, money, relationships, your family, your health, your past, your present, or your future—these thought-seeds are planted in the fertile soil of what we could call Infinite Intelligence, or God. Your life then becomes a reflection of the thought-seeds you've planted in the soil of Infinite Intelligence. Therefore, your life is a reflection of the thoughts you consistently think.

> YOU'RE PLANTING THOUGHT-SEEDS EVERY MOMENT OF YOUR LIFE.

Now, you would think, with the sheer number of books and programs in our industry that support this notion, that by now we'd all know how to change our lives simply by changing our thoughts. But all you have to do is look around to see that unfortunately, that is not the case yet. But why not?

DO TRY THIS AT HOME

In my keynote speeches, private workshops, and live events around the world, I like to do a fun exercise with my audience members. I have everyone stand up and say a traditional "affirmation" like, "I am rich."

So everyone says (with a lot of emotion, because that's what we've been taught to do): "I am rich!"

Guess what happens next? Everyone starts laughing!

I say, "What are you laughing at?"

They say, "But I'm not rich."

I say, "But you just said you were."

And they say, "Yeah, but I don't believe it."

That's why I call it the "Yeah, right" response in the brain—because when you say an affirmation like "I am rich," your brain replies, "Yeah, right!"

The fact is, millions of people have been saying, writing, and repeating these positive statements over and over and over again for years and years and years. Yet we simply don't believe them.

And that lack of belief, which I call **The Belief Gap**, is precisely the problem with the traditional "affirmation" method.

THE BELIEF GAP

Whenever you're trying to change your life—for example, increase your income, find a more fulfilling career, attract your soulmate, improve your health, lose weight, get a new car, etc.—what you're really trying to do is to *create a new reality for yourself.*

I like to explain this phenomenon using the illustration below. What you're really trying to do is go from where you are—what I call your **Current Perceived Reality** (CPR)—to where you want to be, or your **New Desired Reality** (NDR).

Right now, you're living in your *Current Perceived Reality.* In your CPR, you have what you think you have, you know what you think you know, you do what you think you're supposed to do, and you are who you think you are.

However, right now, there are things you want to change about your life. For example, you might want to change your weight, your finances, your health, your relationships, your sphere of influence, the amount of money in your bank accounts, your lifestyle, or any number of things.

That is what I call your *New Desired Reality*—it's your pot of gold at the end of the rainbow. That is where you want to go to and the "new reality" you want to experience.

© and ™ Noah St. John

Between your CPR and your NDR lies what I call your **Belief Gap**—the space between where you believe you are right now (your CPR) and what it will be like when you arrive at your NDR. How big is your Belief Gap? That depends on a number of things; for example:

✓ How long you've been in your CPR

✓ How hard you think it will be to get to your NDR

✓ How many of your friends tell you it's impossible

✓ The kind of support system you have to reach your NDR

…and so on.

Also, you probably have different Belief Gaps for different results in your life. For example, you may think it's really hard to lose 20 pounds but really easy to make an extra $10,000 a month. On the other hand, you may think losing 20 pounds is a piece of cake (pun intended), but to make an extra $10,000 a month is well-nigh impossible.

Bottom line: Until you cross your individual Belief Gap for each result, outcome, or experience that you want, it will be very difficult for you to make the leap to create the new reality you desire.

BRIDGING THE GAP

Have you ever realized you were planting negative thought-seeds—for example, "I'm broke," "I'm lonely," "I can't lose weight"—decided you wanted something better, tried saying positive statements over and over again just like they told us to, and then had absolutely nothing happen? Me too, and about a zillion other people. But the question is, why?

The reason the traditional "affirmation" method did not give us the results we were hoping for is because we were trying to overcome The Belief Gap using only statements—because that's what we were told to do. Yet your subconscious mind, the place where positive changes begin, responds automatically to something that's *both simpler and more powerful than statements.*

The staggering realization I made in the shower on that fateful morning in April 1997 was that you create your life in two ways: by the statements you say to yourself and others; and by the questions you ask yourself and others.

Traditional success teachers told you to change your statements if you want to change your life. That method worked for millions of people, and for millions of people it didn't.

Until The Shower That Changed Everything, no one had fully realized or shown how to harness the awesome power of what happens when you change your internal and external questions.

EMPOWERING VS. DISEMPOWERING QUESTIONS

Most people are going through life asking mostly disempowering questions without realizing it, then wondering why they're not getting the results they dream of. They have developed the unconscious habit of asking disempowering questions, which lead to disempowering actions, which lead to disempowering results.

That's why the first Power Habit is to consciously change your disempowering questions into empowering questions using my Afformations® Method. In short, Power Habit #1 is called **Use Afformations®**.

Therefore, let's begin by examining the disempowering questions you're unconsciously asking right now and then learn how to consciously change them into Afformations, which are empowering questions.

Disempowering questions are questions that do precisely that—they disempower you and effectively *take away your power to act* by focusing your mind on what you *don't* have, what you *can't* do, and who you are *not*. For example:

YOUR MIND RESPONDS AUTOMATICALLY TO SOMETHING EVEN MORE POWERFUL THAN STATEMENTS.

- *Why am I so broke?*
- *Why doesn't anyone love me?*
- *Why isn't my business growing?*
- *Why can't I get the job I want?*
- *Why can't I lose weight?*
- *Why is there more MONTH left at the end of the MONEY?*

These are examples of disempowering questions, because they cause you to believe that you can't do the things that you want to do in life. Of course, no one goes around asking questions like this consciously or on purpose. However, you may be unconsciously asking disempowering questions like these without even realizing it.

As I explain in our seminars and mastermind programs, each of us is carrying around what I call a **Negative Reflection** in our heads. That's

> **WHEN YOU ASK NEGATIVE QUESTIONS, YOU GET NEGATIVE RESULTS.**

the inner voice that tells us we can't do anything right. The *Negative Reflection* always asks negative or disempowering questions like the ones I just mentioned. The ultimate result of these negative or disempowering questions is that you manifest what you focus on. In other words, when you ask negative questions, you get negative results.

Right now, I want you to write five disempowering questions that you ask yourself on a regular basis. Yes, I mean right now. These disempowering questions may have come from someone in your past, or perhaps you made them up on your own. Either way, it's vital that you know exactly what your disempowering questions are, so you can begin to turn them around immediately. Please do this right now. (I'll wait.)

Whew! Pretty bad, aren't they?

Are you ready to try a BETTER way?

AFFORMATIONS® = EMPOWERING QUESTIONS

Now that you've identified some of the disempowering questions you've been unconsciously asking yourself, let's look at how you can start to "flip them" using my AFFORMATIONS METHOD.

Empowering questions are questions that have precisely the opposite effect of disempowering questions. Whereas disempowering questions focus your mind on what you don't have, can't do, and are not—and therefore take away your power to act—*empowering questions* focus your mind on what you DO have, what you CAN do, and Who You Really ARE.

So, let's try something fun right now. I want you to "flip" the disempowering questions you just wrote into empowering questions. How? Simply reverse the negative question to make a positive one!

For example, let's say that one of the disempowering questions you wrote was, "Why do I never get the lucky breaks other people get?"

When you "flip" this disempowering question, your empowering question might be: *Why am I so lucky?*

Or, if one of your disempowering questions was, "Why am I so fat?"—your empowering question could be, *Why is it so easy for me to lose weight?*

Got it?

To turn your disempowering questions into empowering ones, simply "flip" your disempowering questions using the method I just described.

All right, grab your pen, and get ready to experience the Afformations® difference. Ready? Take the five disempowering questions you just wrote in the previous exercise, and "flip" them using my AFFORMATIONS METHOD. Be sure to write the date next to your new Afformations, so you can record the exact date your life (and the universe) changed!

TURN YOUR DISEMPOWERING QUESTIONS INTO EMPOWERING ONES.

Pretty cool, huh?

Did you notice something shift in your mind?

Congratulations, you've just taken the first step in The Power Habits System!

HER $10,000
#AFFORMATIONS SUCCESS STORY

One of my favorite parts of my work is receiving real-life success stories from faithful readers just like you from around the world. (We call ourselves Afformers—use the hashtags **#Afformations** and **#AfformersRock** when you post YOUR story on social media!)

For example, Saqui, an Afformer from London, posted this Afformations Success Story:

> I have made so many incredible life breakthroughs since discovering your #Afformations Method that I've lost count. Here's a recent one: I needed $7,000 to pay a tax bill and of course, as is my habit now, one of my first actions for a problem, need or goal is to #Afform about it. Within a few weeks I attracted a series of things that brought me $10,000 !!!!
>
> I owe everything good in my life at this point to your #Afformations Method. I honestly don't know where I'd be without it!

WHY ARE THEY CALLED AFFORMATIONS®?

One of my favorite subjects in high school was Latin (yes, I was a nerd long before it was cool to be a nerd). After The Shower That Changed Everything, I discovered that the word *affirmation* comes from the Latin word *firmare*, which means "to make firm."

So I asked myself, "If 'affirmations' are positive *statements*, what would be the perfect word to describe *empowering questions?*"

After I asked the question, the answer came to me (of course!).

I realized that whenever we ask questions, whether empowering or disempowering, we are really FORMING thought patterns, which FORM our beliefs, which FORM our habits, which then FORM our very lives.

The word *form* comes from the Latin word *formare*, which means "to form or give shape to." That's when it hit me: What if you're making something FIRM, but it's in the wrong FORM? That would be called *forming a life you didn't want.*

That's when I realized why so many people can't overcome their Belief Gap using only statements—because even though you're trying to make something FIRM, you haven't yet FORMED your new belief structure or new habits. It's like trying to build a house without first pouring the foundation.

I realized that before we make something *firm*, we first need to *form* questions that will change the thought-seeds we're sowing, which will change our thinking, change our beliefs, change our habits, and ultimately change our lives.

And that's how the word and the teaching of AFFORMATIONS® were born.

By the way, it's perfectly legitimate to invent a new word to describe a new technology or a new way of looking at the universe. For example, remember the first time you heard the words *Internet, Google,* or even *computer?* Just a short time ago in human history, these words didn't exist, because the technology they described didn't exist. There was no context for the words—no context, no meaning. Now, of course, we use these words every day.

WHAT IF YOU'RE MAKING SOMETHING FIRM, BUT IT'S IN THE WRONG FORM?

In this book, as well as in my keynote speeches, private workshops and live seminars, I teach you *a new technology of the mind*—hence AFFORMATIONS: a new word to describe a new technology and a new way of looking at the universe.

HOW TO CHANGE YOUR HABITS USING AFFORMATIONS®

Let's go back to our example we've been using. You have a desire to lose weight; that's your GOAL. The new habit you want to adopt to help you reach your goal is drinking more water instead of soda. So your current Habit Loop would look like this:

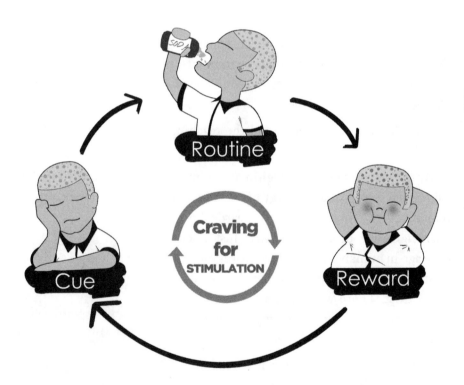

The Habit Loop Causes Craving

Now we're going to add the fifth and final element to the Habit Loop, which is the element called **Belief**. Your Belief represents your *unconscious assumption* about this particular habit. In this case, your Belief might be "It's hard to give up soda."

This Belief leads to more Craving, which leads to the Routine being repeated over and over, which leads to the Belief being even more ingrained in your subconscious, and so on. That's why it's called the Habit **LOOP**—because it keeps going around and around forever, until and unless we *do something different* to change it.

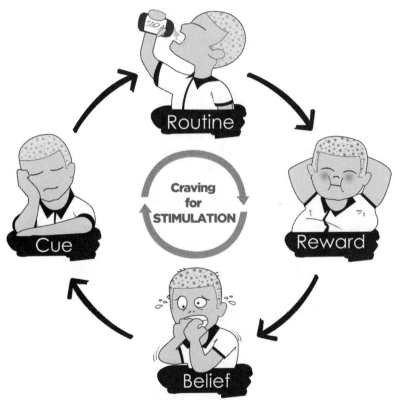

"It's hard to give up soda"

The Habit Loop Builds Belief

USE AFFORMATIONS® IN ALL FOUR MODES OF HUMAN COMMUNICATION.

Now, because we want to form a new habit, we first need to interrupt this pattern. So we're going to *use AFFORMATIONS* to change your subconscious beliefs.

First, **identify the habit you want to change**. In this example, you could write, "I want to drink more water and less soda."

Next, **FORM what you want into an empowering question** that assumes that what you want already has happened or is already true.

So in this example, you could use Afformations like:

- *Why do I love drinking water throughout the day?*
- *Why is it so easy for me to give up soda?*
- *Why am I so healthy?*

Write your own Afformations or use the Recommended Resources at the end of this chapter and the back of this book to help you.

The next step is to give yourself to the question.

This means to read your Afformations, write them, say them out loud, and listen to them. Why are these so important? Because those are the four modes of human communication: reading, writing, speaking, and listening. *Giving yourself to the question* means using all four modes of human communication to change your subconscious thought patterns.

My coaching clients often ask me, "Which communication mode works the fastest?" What they're really asking is, "Which of these should I spend the most time doing?"

While all four modes of human communication are essential, my experience helping people just like you to add six and seven figures to their business—as well as find love, lose weight, gain self-confidence, and more—has shown that *listening to your Afformations* produces the fastest results.

Why? Well, think about it: How many negative thoughts have you had about yourself in your lifetime? A trillion? A billion kajillion? Could we even count that high?

Most of us could hardly count the number of negative thoughts we've had about ourselves. When you think negative thoughts, you are effectively *listening to someone say these things in your head.* That's why I invented **iAfform® Audios**.

YOUR FREE GIFT—MY iAFFORM® AUDIO

iAfform® Audios are done-for-you recordings of empowering Afformations® set to inspiring music. Listening to iAfform Audios helps you change your subconscious thought patterns while you're busy doing other things.

For example, many of my coaching clients listen to their iAfform Audios while they're working, resting, exercising—even while they're sleeping! In fact, I was listening to my iAfform Audios while I was writing this book for you!

Because of the demand from clients around the world, I created iAfform® Audios to help you get better results in all areas of life, including:

✓ Ultimate Wealth

✓ Ultimate Health

✓ Ultimate Love

✓ Ultimate Self-Confidence

✓ Easy Weight Loss

✓ Deep, Blissful Sleep

✓ Living Your Life Purpose

…and many more.

That's why I encourage you to try iAfform Audios by downloading a free 60-Second iAfform® Audio Stress Buster at **www.iAfform.com**.

Yes, you can bust your stress in 60 seconds or less! And remember, it's **<u>FREE</u>**—my gift to you for purchasing this book.

YOUR ASSUMPTIONS FORM YOUR LIFE

Which brings us to the fourth step of my Afformations® Method—the one you absolutely must do if you want Afformations to work for you. And that is: **Take new actions based on your new assumptions about life.**

Right now, you are making hundreds, perhaps thousands, of unconscious assumptions about life and your relationship to it. These assumptions form the basis of how you go through life—positively or negatively, confidently or hesitantly, from love or from fear. However, the problem is that we usually don't recognize our own unconscious assumptions.

For example, let's say that one of your assumptions is, "Things always work out for the best for me." If you hold that assumption, what will your actions be? Right: your actions will tend to be confident, your posture will be self-assured, and you will persist even in the face of temporary failure.

But what if you hold the opposite assumption: "Things never work out for me." If this is the case, your actions will be hesitant, your posture will be one of defeat, and you will tend to give up at the first sign of resistance or rejection.

Which means that no matter what you assume, *you always make yourself right.*

Susan, one of my coaching clients, writes:

> Before working with Noah, I had spent more than $60,000 on "SHELF-help programs" and was about to lose everything—my home, my marriage—and was actually on the verge of bankruptcy. Then I heard about Noah and his methods.
>
> After just 6 months of following Noah's System, I landed my dream job and am now making a 6-figure income doing what I love. In fact, I loved it so much that I became one of Noah's Power Habits® Certified Coaches. Thank you Noah for changing my life!

IT'S NOT MAGIC, IT'S SCIENCE

NO MATTER WHAT YOU ASSUME, YOU ALWAYS MAKE YOURSELF RIGHT.

Over the last two decades, I've had countless thousands of people from around the world tell me that as soon as they started using my Afformations® Method, they felt an immediate feeling of calm and peace wash over them.

Many have seen nearly instantaneous changes in their outlook on life, their emotions, their health, and their habits; and over time, they found themselves manifesting things that had once seemed impossible.

However—and this is a very important point—the Afformations Method is based on science, not magic.

For example, you cannot ask yourself, "Why am I so thin and healthy?" while continuing to eat unhealthy foods and not exercising and expect to lose weight.

You can't Afform "Why is my business so successful?" and never do anything to grow your business and expect it to actually grow—any more than you would expect a plant to grow if it were never watered or nourished.

Bottom line: You cannot break the laws of the universe by asking positive questions and continuing to do negative or self-defeating behaviors and expect to manifest the things you want.

The point of Afformations® is not always to find the answer to your questions. The point is to change what your mind focuses on so that you can build new habits and form a new life.

For example, one of my clients named Tim sent me the following story:

> I'm a consultant for a communications company and had been working with an elderly woman at her house on an issue she had with her home security. Every ten minutes she would go outside to have a cigarette.
>
> After the fourth or fifth time, I asked her if she had ever thought of quitting. She told me, "Every day for the last 20 years."
>
> I asked her what she had tried. The patch, the pill, cold turkey, hypnosis, and so many other things she couldn't even remember. It was obvious to me that even though she didn't like smoking, she just couldn't quit.
>
> I asked her if she would be willing to try just one more thing. She said she would. I wrote this question on a piece of paper and put it on a refrigerator: "Why is it so easy for me to quit smoking this time?" I asked her

to look at it once or twice a day and not to worry about answering it. She said she would.

I planned to check on her again in a couple of weeks but got so busy that I didn't get around to it. About five weeks later, however, she had another issue, and I needed to go to her house again.

> **USE AFFORMATIONS® TO HELP YOU MOVE FROM "IMPOSSIBLE" TO "I'M POSSIBLE."**

I returned to her home and this time was at her house for over one and a half hours, and during all that time she didn't go outside to smoke—not even once.

As I was leaving, I noticed that her smoking area was all cleaned up and there was no evidence of any cigarettes.

I turned and looked at her. She said (and I quote), "I don't know why it was so easy to quit this time." My heart responds, "Wow! This stuff works!" Thanks, Noah.

GUESS WHAT? YOU'RE ALREADY DOING THIS

Remember, my Afformations® Method is based on science, not magic. You cannot break the laws of the universe by sowing positive questions and continuing to do negative or self-defeating habits and expect to reach your goals. The point of Afformations® is not to try and trick your mind, but to use it properly.

Bottom line: You're already using Afformations anyway, but most people are using them in negative, disempowering, or self-defeating ways. Now that you've been exposed to this teaching, you can begin to form new Afformations and use them to help you move from "impossible" to "I'm Possible."

Use them, go over them again and again, and write them out as you would your traditional affirmations—but notice that Afformations may flow much more easily for you!

That's because rather than trying to force yourself to believe something that you don't really believe, you'll be forming new assumptions about life and your relationship to it based on what you really do want.

I know of no other method that can yield such dramatic results with so little effort. Using Afformations, you can take direct, conscious control of your subconscious thoughts—change the questions, change your results, and change your life!

For more information on how to use Afformations to get what you want twice as fast with half the effort, visit **www.Afformations.com**.

NOAH'S NOTES (IN A NUTSHELL)

1. Traditional success teachers told us to use "affirmations" (positive statements) to get the results we wanted. While this worked for some, it left millions of people frustrated, confused, and beating themselves up for not reaching their goals.

2. That's because, while positive statements are great, the human mind operates using questions. When you ask a question, your mind automatically searches for the answer.

3. In 1997, I discovered and named **The AFFORMATIONS® Method**—a new way to ask empowering questions to change your subconscious assumptions and thereby change your life.

4. That's why Power Habit #1 is **Use AFFORMATIONS®**, because using AFFORMATIONS can help you go from your Current Perceived Reality (where you are) to your New Desired Reality (where you want to be) faster, easier, and with a lot less stress.

5. Use the steps in this chapter to begin to use AFFORMATIONS in every area of your life—health, wealth, love, relationships, business, and more.

6. For additional exclusive video training, the Complete AFFORMATIONS Guidebook, ongoing support, and expert interviews, join **The AFFORMATIONS® System** online learning academy at **www.Afformations.com**.

7. Download your free 60-Second Stress Buster and get the complete iAfform® Audio Collection at **www.iAfform.com**. See also the Recommended Resources section at the back of this book for how to use AFFORMATIONS to change your life.

#POWERHABITSCHALLENGE #1

1. For your first Power Habits Challenge, write a post or share a video on social media about the difference between "affirmations" and AFFORMATIONS®, as well as one thing you're going to do from this chapter this week, using the hashtag #PowerHabitsChallenge.

2. Be sure to tag me @NoahStJohn so I'll see your post.

CHAPTER 7

POWER HABIT #2:
ENGAGE YOUR LOVING MIRRORS

"Our character is a composite of our habits. Because they are consistent, often unconscious patterns, our habits constantly express our character."
— Stephen Covey

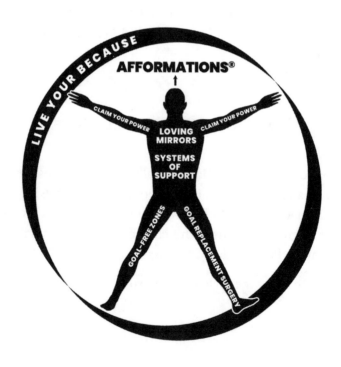

Imagine that right now, you are in your home, looking at yourself in a mirror. What do you see?

While you may have opinions—both positive and negative—about what you see in the mirror, the simple answer is that when you look in a mirror, you see an accurate (albeit two-dimensional) reflection of yourself.

Now imagine that right next to your home, someone has built a funhouse (zoning laws notwithstanding). And you decided to go into said funhouse to have a look around.

What do they put in funhouses? Exactly—funhouse mirrors. And what does a funhouse mirror do? Right—distort the image that's reflected back to you. For example, one funhouse mirror might make you look like you're eight feet tall, while another might make you look like you're three feet tall.

WHAT IF YOU HAD NEVER SEEN AN ACCURATE REFLECTION OF YOURSELF?

Did you actually become eight feet tall or three feet tall when you walked into the funhouse? Of course not. However, because that's the way these funhouse mirrors were designed, that's the image that's reflected back to you.

Now let's continue this imagination exercise…

What if, for some reason, you had never seen your **accurate reflection** in a mirror in your home, and the only reflection you had ever seen of yourself was the **distorted reflection** you saw in a funhouse mirror? In other words, what if you had never seen an *accurate reflection* of yourself—only a *distorted reflection* of yourself—and you had no other way to see what you really looked like?

If this had happened to you—and you had no other way to corroborate this information—you would actually believe that the distorted reflection of you was what you really looked like. That, in turn, would cause you to believe things about yourself that were inaccurate—for instance, that you were either eight feet tall or three feet tall, depending on which funhouse mirror you looked in.

I've shared this analogy with countless thousands of people in my keynote speeches, private workshops, and live seminars, and everyone immediately understands the power of this illustration. I then ask my audience members a simple question that has brought many people, men and women alike, to tears...

"How many of us grew up in the funhouse?"

We humans believe what our senses tell us. The old saying "Seeing is believing" illustrates this principle. This means that if the only information (sensory data) you'd ever received was inaccurate, you'd be forced to believe it.

For example, when I was growing up, my parents argued all the time about money—specifically, the fact that we didn't have any. As I mentioned in an earlier chapter, my mother showed me that there was more MONTH left at the end of the MONEY. So I developed a belief that said, "My family would be better off if I weren't here."

Now of course, my mother did not intend for me to form that belief. Nevertheless, because of that belief, I made every effort to "not be there"—including leaving home at age 15 and deciding to commit suicide at age 25. It was only through a great deal of deep Inner Game work that I was finally able to identify and overcome this long-held belief.

YOUR AUTHENTIC SELF AND YOUR NEGATIVE REFLECTION

The sad truth is that most of us have never seen ourselves accurately reflected by the people around us, even those closest to us. Just as a funhouse mirror distorts your physical reflection, when we receive inaccurate information about Who We Really Are from the people around us, what happens is a distortion of our **Authentic Self**.

Since the beginning of recorded history, human beings have asked ourselves some version of the question, "What is the soul?" And we've come up with many names for this part of us: *soul, spirit, prana, chi, ki, atman, Brahman, energy, Infinite Intelligence, Higher Self,* and so on. I simply choose to call it your *Authentic Self*.

Your Authentic Self is the "still, small voice" that knows that Who You Are is enough. It often speaks to us in dreams or intuition, or that "gut feeling" when you know that something is right.

Yet what happens when your Authentic Self—Who You Really Are—is not accurately reflected back to you, like in the funhouse mirror analogy?

That's when you develop what I call the **Negative Reflection**. Your *Negative Reflection* represents the **head trash** that most of us are carrying around—that voice in your head that says, *You can't do it. Who do you think you are? You'll never be successful.*

In short, your Authentic Self knows you're good enough and that you are capable. Yet your Negative Reflection tells you that you're not good enough and you're not capable. Each of us has our own unique head trash with our own unique negative messages that we tell ourselves. Yet that's not even the real problem.

THE BULLY IN YOUR HEAD

YOUR AUTHENTIC SELF IS THE "STILL, SMALL VOICE" WITHIN.

Many of us have faced bullying throughout our lives. For example, when I was in grade school, a kid named Kevin bullied me. Of course, he was a classic "jock"—naturally gifted at athletics. And of course, I was a nerd long before it was cool to be a nerd—easy pickings for a jock bully.

Today, millions of kids face online bullying—the kind of bullying where the bully doesn't even need to be present to ruin someone's life. In fact, because it's so easy to hide behind a computer screen or smartphone, bullies are finding it easier than ever to make their victim's lives miserable.

When a schoolyard bully demands your lunch money, you face a decision: you can either stand up to the bully or give in to him. If you stand up to the bully, he might beat you up—but he might back down. If, however, you give in to the bully, he will probably keep bullying you, because that's what bullies do.

THE NEGATIVE REFLECTION IS THE BULLY IN YOUR HEAD.

The Negative Reflection is like a bully in your head. It threatens, attacks, and demeans your Authentic Self using a constant barrage of highly targeted criticism that undermines our self-belief.

For example, Cheryl, one of my coaching clients, told me that she felt guilty whenever she took time off from work—and as a result, hadn't taken a real vacation in years. When I asked her why she felt guilty taking time off work, she said it was because she thought she was being "selfish."

Then I asked her what her Negative Reflection was telling her. She replied that her Negative Reflection was telling her that "if you take time for yourself, you're selfish—and when you're 'selfish' it means you're a bad person."

I pointed out that if you take this erroneous message to its logical conclusion, that means you should never do anything for yourself, including eat, sleep, or enjoy life at all.

Cheryl realized that she was being bullied by her Negative Reflection, and shortly after that, she took her first real vacation in more than five years. She even told me that not only did she enjoy her time off, she even enjoyed all the planning and preparation to get ready for the trip—because she heard "the bully in her head" the whole time, and she told it to take a hike!

> A LOVING MIRROR BELIEVES IN YOU BEFORE YOU BELIEVE IN YOURSELF.

By the way, my bullying story ended happily too. When we entered seventh grade, Kevin stopped bullying me and we wound up becoming good friends. I think we finally started to appreciate each other's unique strengths, and we even acted in a school play together. I know that not every bullying story ends happily, but fortunately for us, this one did.

THE LOVING MIRROR PRINCIPLE

If, like many of us, you were raised in an environment where your faults or shortcomings were constantly brought up to you, where the people in your household did not appreciate or accept you for Who You Really Are, or where you were constantly compared to other people and found to come up short—in short, if you were raised in a typical home—it's likely that you developed a Negative Reflection, or head trash.

That's why the second Power Habit is: **Engage Your Loving Mirrors.** A *Loving Mirror* is a person who gives you **unconditional support** and *believes in you before you believe in yourself.*

Have you ever noticed that it's often easier to see positive qualities in other people than in ourselves? For example, it's probably easy for you to see other people as capable, skilled, smart, talented, and competent—yet if I were to ask you if you saw these same qualities in yourself, it might be hard for you to do it.

Why does this happen? One answer is most of us were taught not to think too highly of ourselves—not to boast or brag and not get too big for our britches. (Who wears britches anymore anyway...and why are they always so small?)

The point is, many of us are afraid of being called arrogant or "stuck on ourselves"—and I'm not suggesting you should become either one. However, one critical reason that highly successful people became highly successful is because someone believed in them before they believed in themselves.

Just like you can never see your own eyes without looking in a reflective substance like a mirror or photograph, it's hard to comprehend your true value from within yourself. That's why it takes the loving support and encouragement from someone like a friend, teacher, coach, mentor, or spouse to show you what you're really capable of.

HOW TRADITIONAL SUCCESS TEACHERS SET YOU UP TO FAIL

Here's the problem: I've had the opportunity to interview over 200 highly successful people, including multi-millionaires and icons of industry; and when I asked them exactly how they came to believe in themselves, they finally admitted that they would not have been able to get to where they are without the loving support and encouragement of *someone who believed in them when they didn't even believe in themselves.*

This is one of the great ironies of The Power Habits® System— because the Naturals have been telling us for decades that the secret to success is, "Just believe in yourself."

It's not that believing in yourself is wrong; it's just that when they tell you to "believe in yourself," they got the *order* wrong. That's because *believing in yourself* is actually the final stage, not the first stage, in the evolution of success.

The first stage is *someone believes in you.*

The second stage is *you believe in someone else.*

The final stage is *you believe in yourself.*

We are often the worst judge of what we're really capable of. Aren't we sometimes our own worst enemy? Well, if what you want is love, support, and encouragement, is it really smart to go to your worst enemy?

THE NATURALS JUST KEPT TELLING US TO "BELIEVE IN YOURSELF."

Bottom line: You are probably the least capable person to know what you are truly capable of. That's why the Loving Mirror Principle I teach my coaching clients and in my live seminars is the exact opposite of what they taught us in traditional success programs.

HOW TO BEAT THE BULLY IN YOUR HEAD

But you might say, "Noah, this sounds great, but I don't have anyone who believes in me. I don't have a Loving Mirror." That's the #1 objection I hear when I teach this Power Habit in my keynote speeches and workshops. Yet that's the very point.

If you weren't lucky enough to have been born into a family of Loving Mirrors (as most of us weren't), you can now install this new Power Habit and engage your Loving Mirrors, even if you've never had them before.

So let's start at the beginning by going back to our Habit Loop that we learned in an earlier chapter. Remember the five elements that make up the Habit Loop: Cue, Routine, Reward, Craving, and Belief. Now I want you to do this simple but astonishingly powerful five-step exercise I call *Identify Your Head Trash Triggers*.

Step 1: Write the Cue that triggers your head trash. Let's go back to our example of wanting to lose weight and get in shape. Your Cue in this case has been the feeling of boredom or stress or thirst that comes up during your day. So in this step, you would write: "My Cue is that I feel bored or stressed."

Step 2: Write the Routine you're currently doing when the Cue is triggered. In this case, your Routine is reaching for the can of soda, so you'd write: "I drink soda when this Cue is triggered."

Step 3: Write the Reward you get when you do this Routine. In this example, your Reward is the feeling of being satisfied that comes after drinking soda. So you'd write: "I feel satisfied after I drink soda."

Step 4: Write the Belief that's installed when you do this habit. In this case, you might write, "I believe that it's hard for me to give up drinking soda."

Step 5: Write the Negative Reflection message you hear as a result of this Belief. For example, since you believe it's hard to give up drinking soda, your Negative Reflection might pile on with a message like, "You're stupid and weak and can't do anything right." (Boy, he's mean. I told you he was a bully.)

Go ahead and do this exercise right now, for the habit you'd like to change. (I'll wait.)

So how do we use this information to change our habit? Well, the first thing we're going to do is *replace the old Routine with a new one.*

HOW TO CHANGE ANY HABIT WITHOUT USING WILLPOWER

You see, while a habit is comprised of these five basic elements, most people fail because they try to use "willpower" to change their habits. Yet willpower, as it's taught by most traditional success teachers, is basically you yelling at yourself to change! And while that can work for a short time, it's also the main reason why most attempts to change our behavior fail—not because we're weak, but because we're trying to use a weak part of ourselves to make the change. It's like trying to change a tire on your car by trying to lift the car with your bare hands.

So rather than trying to do something that's bound to fail, let me give you a simple exercise that can help you beat the bully in your head—a *lever* that will empower you to make massive changes without having to use willpower. I call this exercise ***How to Change Any Habit Without Using Willpower.***

Step 1: Write the Cue that triggers your head trash.

This is the same Cue from the head trash exercise you just did. So in this step, you would again write: "My Cue is that I feel bored or stressed."

Step 2: List all possible new Routines you can do when this Cue is triggered.

This is one of the major differences of The Power Habits System. Traditional behavior modification systems told us to simply "stop doing that" when it comes to habits that we want to change. Yet once a habit becomes a habit, trying to "stop" doing it usually doesn't work. You can, however, ***replace that habit*** with something else, something better, something more productive for you. And the place to start is with your Routine.

So now I want you to list all the possible new Routines that you could do to *replace* the one you're currently doing that doesn't serve you.

Using our example, when you feel bored or stressed or thirsty, instead of reaching for a can of soda, what could you do? Well, you could...

✓ Reach for a glass of water

✓ Reach for an apple, orange, or other healthy fruit

✓ Reach for almonds, pecans, or other healthy nuts (most fruits and nuts have a natural sweet taste that will satiate your brain's desire for sweets, yet are far healthier for you)

✓ Call one of your Loving Mirrors (see also the exercise below)

✓ Read your new Afformations®

✓ Listen to your iAfform® Audios

✓ Say your new healthy Afformations out loud

The truth is, there are dozens of things you can do to replace your old, disempowering habit with a new, empowering habit. List them here.

Step 3: List the Rewards you're going to get when you do this new, empowering Routine.

For example, your Rewards when you do these new, healthy Routines could include...

✓ Greater self-esteem

✓ More self-confidence

✓ Feeling empowered

✓ Being happier

✓ Losing weight

✓ Looking sexier

✓ Feeling better about yourself when you look in the mirror

Are you starting to see how this works?

Step 4: Write your new Beliefs in the form of AFFORMATIONS®.

For instance, your new AFFORMATIONS could include...

✓ Why is it so easy for me to lose weight?

✓ Why do I love having healthy habits?

✓ Why was it so easy for me to give up soda?

✓ Why do I love what I see when I look in the mirror?

Use the Recommended Resources from the previous chapter and at the back of this book to help you create your own empowering Afformations.

Step 5: Write the message you hear from your Authentic Self when you install these new Beliefs and new Afformations.

Now that you've stood up to the bully in your head, you might be able to more clearly hear the "still, small voice" of your Authentic Self. Write what you hear from that voice. It could be messages like:

✓ I can do this.

✓ I am enough.

✓ I'm more than capable.

✓ I'm stronger than I thought I was.

Yes, I realize that those are technically "affirmations." However, using my Power Habits System, you're no longer going to be using these statements to try and convince yourself of something you don't believe. Instead, you're going to use my AFFORMATIONS® Method to change your beliefs (Step 4), and then *listen* to the voice of your Authentic Self, the part of you that knows Who You Really Are and is no longer going to be bullied (Step 5). See the difference?

HOW TO ENGAGE YOUR LOVING MIRRORS

Now let's go back to the objection I talked about earlier, which is that "I don't have any Loving Mirrors." Remember, this Power Habit is called *Engage Your Loving Mirrors*, not "Think About Engaging Your Loving Mirrors."

The question is, what should you say when trying to engage someone's support? What shouldn't you say? What's the proper etiquette here? How are other people going to react when you do this?

What I tell my coaching clients and share in my workshops and keynote speeches is that when you're asking for support from another person, you want to be as truthful and transparent as possible.

So here's how you can start...

Step 1: List your potential Loving Mirrors. These should be people you already know who may be able to provide you with the kind of support that I'm describing in this chapter.

Step 2: Reach out to each potential Loving Mirror. This should be in the form of a phone call, face-to-face, email, text, or messenger. Reach out in whatever way seems appropriate for each individual.

I recommend that you say (communicate) something like this: "(NAME), you're a very important person to me. I'm making some big changes in my life, and I'd like you to be a part of it. Right now, I'm reading a book called *Power Habits* by an author named Noah St. John. He told us to interview the most important people in our lives, because he said that highly successful people have people who believe in them. Noah calls these people Loving Mirrors, and I was wondering if this is something you might be open to."

Now, your friend might say, "What are you talking about?" so just explain what a Loving Mirror is in your own words, or you can even read from this book.

Step 3: Interview your Loving Mirrors. I've given you my Loving Mirror Suggested Interview Questions below. In this step, you're going to "take the temperature of your relationship" using the method I describe below.

You can introduce this step by saying something like this: "I was wondering if I could ask you these questions from the *Power Habits* book. Would that be okay with you?"

By the way, the reason I suggest you refer to this book is twofold: one, because it might feel uncomfortable or even awkward to be this vulnerable to people, if you've never done it before; and two, because when you present it like, "Noah told me to do this," it's kind of like saying your doctor prescribed this course of action—having these things come from an objective third party can often make it easier.

JUST TELL THEM, "NOAH TOLD ME TO DO THIS."

You can interview your Loving Mirrors in person or on the phone. Naturally, with today's technology, you can have Loving Mirrors on the other side of the planet just as easily as the other side of the street.

Here are my suggested Loving Mirror Interview Questions:

1. What do you get out of me being in your life?

2. What have you gained from our relationship?

3. What would be missing if I weren't in your life?

4. What do you see my strengths as being?

5. What can I do differently to improve our relationship?

6. If there were one word or phrase that you'd use to describe our relationship, what would it be?

7. On a scale from 1 to 10, how would you rate our relationship?

8. If anything less than a 10, what can I do to make it a 10?

9. Would it be okay with you if we talked more regularly, so we can support each other's projects and goals?

These questions are very straightforward, but I want to especially bring your attention to questions #7 and #8. My good friend Jack Canfield taught me these two questions, and I think they're two of the most brilliant questions when it comes to human relationships.

I also recommend to my coaching clients that they ask their team members, employees, and even their vendors these two questions on at least a quarterly basis. Why? Because with the people with whom you work, it's easy to "get lazy" and assume that everything's fine—when in fact, they may be harboring things that they're afraid to talk about. Giving them space to talk about these issues can be one of the best things you'll ever do for your personal, as well as your business, relationships.

For example, Elizabeth, an entrepreneur from Portland, Oregon writes:

> When I first came across Noah's work, I'd just started my business and I was confronted with all the "head trash" that comes along with being a new entrepreneur: uncertainty, who-am-I-to-do-this and a TON of fear. I was barely keeping my head above water—emotionally and financially too. Noah's work came along at a pivotal moment in my life. Today, my company is approaching its first million-dollar year. I will always be grateful to Noah for shining his light and putting his work into the world— it reached me at just the right time!

WATCH YOUR "COME-FROM"

When you're Engaging Your Loving Mirrors, where you come from is more important than the questions you ask. I don't mean where you come from geographically; I'm talking about emotionally. That's because you must come from *a place of authenticity* and not neediness when you Engage Your Loving Mirrors.

Coming from a place of not-neediness essentially comes down to two words: ***don't defend***. Why? Because when you ask these kinds of honest questions, you're probably going to get honest answers—some of which you might not necessarily want to hear. And remember that ancient phrase: *The truth hurts.*

We all think we're doing great in our relationships and that the other person will forgive us when we screw up. There's a great quote I like to remember when it comes to human relationships: "We judge ourselves by our intentions, yet we judge others by their actions."

> WE JUDGE OURSELVES BY OUR INTENTIONS, YET WE JUDGE OTHERS BY THEIR ACTIONS.

So the natural thing, when we hear feedback we don't like, is to get defensive. There's just one problem: if you get defensive, you will lose that person's trust, and it will be very hard to gain it back.

For example, let's say you ask someone on your team, "On a scale from 1 to 10, what would you rate our relationship?" They say, "Well, I'd give it a 4." Then you react defensively: "Four! What do you mean 4? I'm always doing things for you. I'm always nice to you…blah blah blah."

If you defend like that, you've lost. Although you may not like what the other person is saying and even completely disagree with it, it's their opinion—and they're just as entitled to their opinion as you are to yours. Here's the truth:

EVERY HUMAN BEING IS SILENTLY ACHING FOR THE CHANCE TO BE HEARD AND NOT BE MADE WRONG.

Everyone is dying to tell their story, and everyone has a story—and to them, it's the truth. *Perception is reality to the perceiver.* So, what if you become the one person who doesn't make people wrong for sharing their opinion? I'm not suggesting you have to agree with everything that everybody says; but you don't have to make them wrong either.

Here's all you have to do when you hear feedback that's hard to hear: First, take a deep breath. They didn't just shoot you with a gun; all they did was tell you something you didn't want to hear.

Then, calmly reflect what they said back to them.

For example, you might say something like, "Okay, you gave our relationship a 4. Hmmm, that's not very good, is it? Why don't you tell me why you'd rate it a 4?"

See what you did there? You gave the other person **permission to tell you the truth.** You didn't make them wrong. You didn't defend. You didn't give excuses. This is the first and most important step to improving your relationships.

GIVE PEOPLE PERMISSION TO TELL YOU THE TRUTH.

Now they might say something like, "Well, you never listen to me. You interrupt me all the time. You didn't let me finish telling you that story."

This is your moment of truth. If you can let them tell their story without defending yourself and without making them wrong, then you've won. All you have to do is *listen*

146

without making them wrong. I say it's "all you have to do"—but boy, is it difficult to actually do.

Then, when they're done telling their side of the story, you can say something like, "Wow, I had no idea I was doing that. Thank you for telling me about it. I'll make sure to do better next time."

And here's the key: You actually have to do better next time!

Because even if you listen to them, even if you don't make them wrong, even if you make them feel heard, if you don't make the change that you promised, then you've caused even more damage to the relationship—and that damage might turn out to be irreparable.

Yes, I know that not defending yourself in the heat of the moment is hard. That's because we all want to be right. But if you can do this without being defensive, you'll find that not only will you increase your self-esteem and self-confidence; you'll also gain the confidence of the people around you, and they'll be much more likely to support you in the long run.

IF YOU NEED SUPPORT, DO THIS

I've just shared a simple yet powerful exercise to Engage Your Loving Mirrors in your life. But what if you need more support than the people in your life can give you? What if you have big dreams and goals that require additional support or guidance?

All you have to do is reach out to our offices here in North America, because we've helped countless thousands of individuals, teams, and companies to install The Power Habits® System in their organizations to the benefit of all.

To book a private workshop for your team, company, or organization, visit **www.NoahStJohn.com/private-workshop**

To have me speak at your next event, visit **www.BookNoah.com**.

And here's one additional thought on the Loving Mirror Principle: Every other "how-to-succeed" program implicitly tells you to go to yourself to find the strength to complete it—in other words, just grit your teeth and get through it.

However, most people don't believe in themselves enough to finish what they started in the first place. That's why, when you Engage Your Loving Mirrors, you'll start to realize that you don't need to depend on your own willpower to get your foot off the brake.

In working with elite coaching clients and mastermind students from around the world for more than two decades, I have found that as we give ourselves *Permission to Succeed*® at higher and higher levels, we need even more support the higher we go.

That's why The Power Habits System is the only business and personal growth system that has the "fail-safe" built right into it. Because when you install this Power Habit, you won't have to depend on your own willpower or motivation or psych yourself up anymore—because, as you now know, these are very limited resources to begin with.

Engage Your Loving Mirrors and allow others to support you on your journey to a more abundant lifestyle. Then you'll have the added benefit of being better able to support others on their journey as well!

NOAH'S NOTES (IN A NUTSHELL)

1. Traditional success teachers told us that the secret of success is to "believe in yourself." While this isn't wrong per se, the truth is that believing in yourself is actually the final stage of belief.

2. That's because every Unconsciously Successful Person had someone believe in them first. I call this person a **Loving Mirror**.

3. **The Loving Mirror Principle** states that human beings believe in themselves when someone believes in them first.

4. That's why Power Habit #2 is **Engage Your Loving Mirrors**, because rather than trying to "believe in yourself," it's a lot easier to succeed when someone believes in you.

5. Your **Negative Reflection** is like a bully in your head—that voice that tells you that you're "not enough," no matter how much you do.

6. Use the exercises in this chapter to Engage Your Loving Mirrors and begin to beat the bully in your head.

7. To book a private workshop for your team, company, or organization, visit:
www.NoahStJohn.com/private-workshop

#POWERHABITSCHALLENGE #2

1. For your second Power Habits Challenge, write a post or share a video about why Loving Mirrors are important to your success using the hashtag #PowerHabitsChallenge. Include one thing you're going to do from this chapter this week.

2. Be sure to tag me @NoahStJohn so I'll see your post.

CHAPTER 8

POWER HABIT #3: UPGRADE YOUR PEOPLE SYSTEM

"Make it a habit to tell people 'thank you.' Express your appreciation sincerely and without the expectation of anything in return. Appreciate those around you, and you'll soon find many others around you."
— Ralph Marston

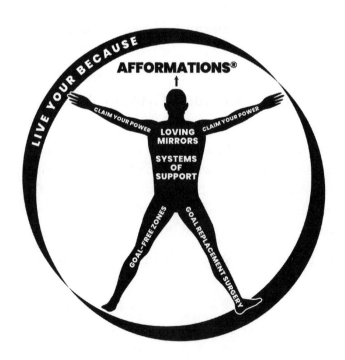

I'd like you to think for a moment about your house. What is your house? Well, your house is a place for you to live, a place you call home, or as George Carlin said, "a place to keep your stuff."

Fundamentally, however, your house is really just two things: **Structure** and **Systems**. For instance, every house has a basic *Structure*—that is, the arrangement of and relations between the different parts of your house, including the number of rooms, how big each room is, where they're placed, and so forth. That's the Structure of your house.

Secondly, your house consists of *Systems*—a set of things that work together to serve a particular function. Your house's Systems include things like the electrical system, heating system, ventilation system, plumbing system, and so forth.

These interconnected Systems make your house function as a place where you can live comfortably. That is *the function of a house.* However, if your house's Systems don't work properly or work together, instead of a house, you've got a building sitting there that's not much fun to live in.

When is the only time you ever think about the Systems in your house? Exactly—when they're not working properly! For example, the only time you ever think about your plumbing is when your drain is stopped up. You never think about electricity until the power goes out.

Now think about your body. Your body is like a house, because your body is also composed of those same two components: Structure and Systems. The Structure of your body is your basic makeup—whether you're male or female, tall or short, and your individual features and genetic characteristics.

Your body also consists of Systems. The function of your body's Systems is for you to remain alive (i.e., not die). Your body contains dozens of interdependent Systems: circulatory, muscular, skeletal, nervous, respiratory, immune...plumbing!

And just like your house, when is the only time you ever think about these Systems? You got it—when they're not functioning properly. For

YOU ONLY THINK ABOUT YOUR SYSTEMS WHEN THEY'RE NOT WORKING.

instance, you never think about your respiratory system unless you suddenly can't breathe. You never think about your, ahem, plumbing System until something gets, shall we say, stopped up in there.

The point is, if the Systems of your house or your body aren't working at optimal levels, you have a bunch of parts that don't serve the function that you want. With your house, you've got a building that's pretty drafty and uncomfortable to live in; and in the case of your body, you're anywhere from mildly uncomfortable to, um, dead.

THE THREE CAUSES OF STUCKNESS

It's the same with your life and your business. Your life and your business also consist of Structure and Systems, but here's the problem—three problems, actually:

Problem #1: Most people don't know what the Systems of their life or business are. They just have a vague sense that "something's wrong" or they're "stuck."

Problem #2: Since they don't know what the Systems are, they don't know where to start when something's not working.

Problem #3: Since they don't know where to start, they're spending lots of time, money, and effort in the wrong place and getting frustrated with their lack of results.

Imagine if you treated your house like you treated your life or your business. For instance, many people, when they feel "stuck" or want to fix something in their lives or businesses, feel overwhelmed, confused, and don't know where to turn for help. So they ask their friends or go online searching for the latest and greatest fad or "gimmick of the month."

They see this "guru" claiming that they made a gazillion dollars in their underwear just by pushing a button and "you can too!" So they sign up for the guru's program, and when they get it, they realize that the guru made it sound a lot easier than it actually is. They get frustrated, angry, and cynical, because they were lied to by the gurus.

I'll bet you've seen this happen in your own life or in the life of someone you know. I've already shared with you that I paid the "gurus" more than $500,000 over the course of my career and ended up with little or nothing to show for it.

The problem is that when we do things like this, we're usually searching in the wrong place. It's like calling a plumber when you've got an electrical problem. The plumber may have a good solution for a plumbing problem; but if you've got a problem with your electrical system, a plumber won't really be much help.

WHAT'S THE PURPOSE OF YOUR LIFE?

Going back to our house analogy, the purpose of your house is to give you a place to live comfortably. The two questions then, are:

1. What is the purpose of your life?

2. What is the purpose of your business?

I'm going to talk more about your life purpose in Chapter 16; however, whether I'm coaching celebrities, professional athletes,

IF YOU'VE BEEN BURNED BY THE "GURUS," YOU'RE NOT ALONE.

CEOs, working couples, or entrepreneurs, it seems to me that the highest function of an individual's life is *to live in the manner in which you choose and to provide value to others.* That means to be able to choose the lifestyle that you desire and to provide value to others in the form of service or work.

> YOUR BUSINESS EXISTS TO SERVE <u>YOU</u>, NOT THE OTHER WAY AROUND.

Furthermore, I believe that the essential function of your business is to *provide value to a set of human beings and realize a profit from that activity.* Whether you currently own your business or work for someone else, the only way to make money is to *provide value* to a set of human beings and then to profit from that activity. Yet the greater or ultimate function of your business is *to serve your individual lifestyle goals, so you can have the freedom to do more of what you desire to do.*

As you can see from these descriptions, most people are not living what we at SuccessClinic.com call a **Freedom Lifestyle**. And most businesses are certainly not functioning at the level they could, as evidenced by the fact that most business fail after less than five years.

I believe that most people have a vague sense that "something's wrong" and are running around, working really hard, trying to fix the problem. Yet if you had a toothache and went to a knee surgeon to fix it, how successful would that operation be?

THE FIVE ESSENTIAL SYSTEMS OF SUPPORT

I've got some great news for you: *You can stop running around now.*

Why? Because after more than two decades of helping people just like you to add six, and seven (and even eight) figures in sales—as well as find love, be happier, and achieve peace of mind and well-being—I've identified **the Five Essential Systems of Support** you need to have operating properly in order to have the "Freedom Lifestyle" you desire.

The Five Essential Systems of Support are:

1. Your People System

2. Your Activities System

3. Your Environment System

4. Your Introspection System

5. Your Simplify System

These are the five interdependent Systems of Support for your life and your business. And even though they are all interconnected and interdependent, just like your house and your body, each System has its own individual set of rules and requires its own set of habits to keep them operating at optimal levels. Taken together, however, these Systems comprise Power Habits #3 through #7.

The Systems of Support

As we discuss each one, you'll notice that the same Systems that need to be working properly in your life also need to be working properly in your business or your career. This makes studying and installing these Systems much easier, because it means that we can study the same Systems and habits for both your life and your business, rather than having to worry about different sets of Systems for each.

In addition, it doesn't matter if you're married or single, old or young, whether you're an entrepreneur or work for someone else—the Systems remain the same. I know this because I've been privileged to coach, mentor, and work with tens of thousands of individuals, teams, and organizations in my keynote speeches, private workshops, live seminars, and mastermind programs.

So no matter who you are; what your background, level of education, or age is; or even what you want to accomplish, *the Systems remain the same.* However, this also means that if *even one* of these Systems is not working properly, not only will your income suffer, but so will your health, your peace of mind, your well-being, your relationships, and ultimately, your legacy.

WHY YOUR PEOPLE SYSTEM COMES FIRST

Let's begin our journey through Systems of Support with **Power Habit #3: Upgrade Your People System.** Your *People System* consists of everything in your life that has to do with your relationships with other people—every relationship from your spouse, your family and friends, to your employees and customers, vendors and suppliers, colleagues and coworkers.

Why does Upgrading Your People System come first when we discuss success and Power Habits? There are many reasons for this, but the bottom line is this: *because human beings run everything on Earth.*

HOW CAN YOU GROW YOUR BUSINESS WITHOUT THE HELP OF OTHER PEOPLE?

To better understand why Upgrading Your People System is so essential to your success, let's imagine what would happen if you *didn't* do it—that is, if you decide that you're NOT going to Upgrade Your People System.

Let's say you own a business. Who, exactly, is going to buy your products or services? Who, exactly, is going to promote you if you don't have good relationships with your customers and employees? Who, exactly, are you having relationships with, if not the people in your life?

Now I know this might sound almost too simplistic. You might say, "Come on Noah, I know I need to treat people right. Tell me something I *don't* know!"

Oh, really? So your relationships with the people in your life couldn't get any better, huh? You couldn't use more customers, more clients, more leads, more sales, more influencers promoting you and your business?

"Well," you say, looking down and shuffling your shoes, "of course I want that. But you're just talking about marketing, aren't you?"

Hmm, let me see—when you're marketing your products and services, who, exactly, are you marketing to—chimpanzees? Gorillas? Orangutans? (Look, with a name like Noah, I could go on for a while here.)

Of course, you need to market your business in order to grow it. That's one reason we created live events like our Freedom Lifestyle

Experience and Impact Influencer Summit, as well as our Platinum and VIP Coaching programs. (You can learn more about these and other programs in the Recommended Resources section at the back of this book.) Yet isn't it true that really effective marketing happens when one person influences another person or group of people to buy or do something? In other words, "word of mouth" is by far the most effective marketing method—and that means *people interacting with other people.*

As you'll see in this chapter, the truth is that no matter how successful you are right now, you need to have people in your life who can help you get where you want to go—and you do this by Upgrading Your People System. This is what highly successful people do—what they've always done—and it's the essence of this Power Habit.

THE 5 B.A.S.I.C. PEOPLE SYSTEM HABITS

There are what I call **mini-habits** that make up this Power Habit of Upgrading Your People System. A *mini-habit* means one of the little things you do every day that creates big results. As the saying goes, "Big doors swing on small hinges." And the beautiful thing is, when you look at the five mini-habits of the People System, the acronym actually spells the word B.A.S.I.C. They are:

1. **Be** accountable to your Loving Mirrors.

2. **A**sk for the support you need.

3. **S**eek to add value first.

4. **I**nstall Fail-Safes.

5. **C**atch people doing something right.

Let's go through each one in turn...

B.A.S.I.C. People System Habit #1:
Be Accountable to Your Loving Mirrors

In the previous Power Habit, you identified your Loving Mirrors. Now, you're going to make it a habit to be accountable to them on a daily, weekly, monthly, and ongoing basis. Why is this so important? *Because we human beings hate letting other people down.*

Most of us perform best in an environment of **unconditional support**. That means, when someone believes in us and holds us to a higher standard, we begin to hold ourselves to that higher standard that they're holding us to, and that makes us perform at higher levels than we ever thought we could, which means we can create better results than we ever thought possible.

Think about when you hire a coach or a mentor. When you hire them, you give that mentor your trust. That means you trust their judgment and don't want to let them down, because they believe in you. That's why, when you feel accountable to someone else, you will do more than you thought you could, which leads to better habits, better results, and a better life. That's why the habit of being accountable to your Loving Mirrors is so essential to your success.

> HUMANS PERFORM BEST IN AN ENVIRONMENT OF UNCONDITIONAL SUPPORT.

So, how do you install this habit? One simple way is to develop what I call **The Weekly Checklist Habit**. First, create a written checklist of the things that you want to do or complete by the end of the week. Then, email your checklist to your Loving Mirror on Monday.

At the end of the week, tally up what you did, and then send them your end-of-the-week report showing what you completed, any roadblocks you're facing, and what still needs to be done. Doing this will

UNCONSCIOUSLY SUCCESSFUL PEOPLE HAVE NO PROBLEM ASKING FOR HELP.

reinforce in your brain that you are accountable to someone else for getting things done.

Ironically, most human beings will do more when they feel accountable to someone else than they will for themselves. Use this fundamental principle of human behavior to help you get more done, and install this first habit of your People System.

B.A.S.I.C. People System Habit #2: Ask for the Support You Need

Imagine that you and I are in a meeting room with many other people gathered together to study these Power Habits. (In fact, this is what happens in our live seminars, so be sure to join us so you can see for yourself.) Would you find it difficult to ask the people in this room for help? Would you feel embarrassed, shy, or hesitant to ask for the support you need, even from people you know, like, and trust? When I ask this question in my live events and keynote speeches, more than half of the hands in the room go up. Why are we so afraid to ask for the help we need?

The reason is because *we're afraid of rejection.* It's the fear that the other person will turn down our request and then we'll feel inadequate or not good enough. If you're afraid that people will reject you when you ask for the support, then you'll find reasons to keep not asking. However, Unconsciously Successful People have no problem asking for the support they need—even if they don't get it every time.

You've heard it said that the world's best salespeople just keep asking for the sale—not that they hound people; they just keep asking. Now, there is a huge difference between hounding someone and asking for support. You might say, "Well, I don't want to be rude. I don't want to bother people." And you're right—you shouldn't be rude or bother people. But what if by asking, you're presenting an opportunity that would really benefit that other person? If you are adding value to the lives of others, don't you owe it to them, as well as to yourself, to at least see if they're open to the idea?

For example, a colleague who attended one of my seminars told me that the company she worked for could really use my help. She gave me the name of a person to call at the company's headquarters. I called this person and told her what my friend had said. Since my friend was highly respected in the company, I thought that would have a lot of clout.

But the person on the phone said (rather rudely), "No thanks, we're all set," and hung up on me. I thought, "Well, maybe I caught her on a bad day," so I called back a month or so later to try again. "No thanks," click—same response.

I thought this was very odd, so I called my friend back and said, "Are you sure I'm talking to the right person?" My friend then gave me the name of a different person, a vice president who oversaw the company's regional conventions. I called this new person, even though I was mentally prepared to get rejected again. The vice president asked me what I did. I said, "I teach people how to start making a lot more money while working less so they can spend more time with their families." She then asked me how my system works. I told her that my system has helped me and my clients more than $2.2 billion in sales.

She said, "Yes, that sounds good. Let me call you back in a few days." After my experience with the first person, I must admit I really didn't think she was going to call me back.

However, the very next day, that vice president left a message on my phone: "Noah, we'd like you to speak on a cruise to Mexico for 2,000 of our international salespeople. We'll fly you first class to Los Angeles, and you speak for a couple of hours. Then you can relax for the rest of the

> **I DIDN'T THINK SHE'D CALL ME BACK.**

four-day cruise. Oh, and we're also going to put you in the master cabin on the ship and pay for everything. Call my office, and we'll work out the details."

All righty then!

The point of the story is if I had stopped at the first "no," I wouldn't have gotten the chance to speak on that cruise to Mexico, help thousands of people, and get paid to do what I love. However, when I didn't get the result that I wanted initially, *I changed who I asked and how I asked* until I got the result I wanted.

Many teachers talk about how important it is to keep asking and be persistent, and that's true; but what they neglected to tell us is *what causes the habit of persistence.* As discussed in an earlier chapter, you can't change behavior at the level of behavior. That's why it's crucial to ask for the support you need, and when you run into rejection, change who you ask and what you're asking until you get what you're looking for.

B.A.S.I.C. People System Habit #3:
Seek to Add Value First

Every person you will ever meet is wearing an invisible sign that says, "Please make me feel important." The problem is, *you have that sign too.* That's why we're all waiting for the other person to go first and make us feel important, before we'll do it for the other person.

Therefore, consciously *seek to be the person who adds value first.* Because if you can be that one person in a million who makes the other person feel important first, then people will begin to be drawn to you—because human beings like to feel important. This is the habit of your People System I call **Seek to Add Value First**.

How do you do this? One way is to simply ask the question, "What can I do for you?" or "How can I help you?" One of my favorite ways to Seek to Add Value First is to ask the person I'm talking to, "What are you most passionate about these days?"

When you ask this question, two things generally happen: First, you perform a pattern interrupt on the other person. That's because most human interactions follow certain patterns—for example, at a party or networking event, usually a polite conversation like "What do you do for work?" and "Isn't it nice weather we're having?" All of which is fine, but it's also very expected, which is another way to say "boring." That's why asking a *pattern interrupt question* is a great way to get the conversation flowing.

The second thing that happens is that because you're interrupting the normal pattern, you are virtually guaranteed a response that's outside of the norm, and that tends to raise your perceived value in the eyes of the other person.

For example, I've asked everyone from my celebrity clients to people I've just met at a networking event the question "What are you most passionate about these days?" and it never fails to get an interesting response. The point is to develop the habit of seeking to add value first, and you'll find that people will be much more willing to help you than you might think. As my friend Harvey Mackay likes to say, "Dig your well before you're thirsty."

> **SEEK TO ADD VALUE FIRST USING A "PATTERN INTERRUPT."**

B.A.S.I.C. People System Habit #4:
Install Fail-Safes

In literal terms, a *fail-safe* is a device that, in the event of a system failure, responds in a way that will cause the least amount of harm to other devices or people in human terms. In The Power Habits System, **Install Fail-Safes** means realizing that we human beings sometimes fall short of what we're trying to do and therefore must take preventative measures ahead of time to ensure that when we fail or fall short, there is the least amount of damage to ourselves and to others.

INSTALL FAIL-SAFES FOR YOUR LIFE AND YOUR BUSINESS.

One of the most famous and successful examples of a Fail-Safe System is the 12-step structure of Alcoholics Anonymous. AA is a global community of people who come together to support one another in overcoming alcoholism and achieving sobriety. Its support structure consists of The 12 Steps that were laid out by founding members Bill Wilson and Dr. Bob Smith of Akron, Ohio.

The 12 steps are one of the most successful behavior modification programs in human history, and what's truly remarkable about The 12 Steps themselves is that they are a system of interconnected fail-safes, starting with the first step itself: *We admitted that we were powerless over alcohol.*

Bill Wilson and Dr. Bob realized that trying to achieve sobriety through willpower alone had a very small chance of success in the long run. That's why The 12 Steps encourage people to come to believe in something greater than themselves and to rely on the support of the group itself, rather than trying to change their habits using willpower alone.

There's no question that Installing Fail-Safes is not only useful for overcoming addiction; it's also essential for our daily lives. Why? Because the pull of our old habits can be very strong, as we've seen in our studies of neuroscience and the brain itself. That's why Installing Fail-Safes in your life and in your daily routine can often mean the difference between success and failure.

What are some Fail-Safes you can install in your daily life? One example would be to examine the Habit Loops that are currently taking place in your life and realize the specific situations where you're having trouble making the changes you want.

Then, rather than relying only on your willpower to replace your old Routine with a new one, you can Install Fail-Safes like make a phone call, talk with a friend, get up and go for a walk, use Afformations®, and so forth. The purpose of Installing Fail-Safes in your life is to ensure that you don't have to try to make these positive changes alone using only your willpower. Developing this habit will help to ensure your progress and keep you on track to your destination.

B.A.S.I.C. People System Habit #5: Catch People Doing Something Right

The final B.A.S.I.C. People System habit is to **Catch People Doing Something Right**. Why is this so important? Because human beings— you know, those weird creatures who run everything—are starving for attention, appreciation, recognition, and acknowledgment.

Think about how different this habit is from what most people do. Most people are going around catching everyone doing things *wrong* every day. The average person is almost completely focused on what's wrong with their lives. When you're focused on something, what do you find? Right: You find what you're focusing on. (Another way to say this is: What you focus on, grows.)

Therefore, most people have no trouble finding plenty of things wrong with the people and situations in their lives— and they're sure to point it out to everyone every day! Imagine how your life would change if you replaced this one habit of catching people doing things WRONG with the habit of catching people doing things RIGHT.

REPLACING THIS ONE HABIT CAN WORK WONDERS FOR YOU.

For example, I used to be a highly critical person, because I was so critical and judgmental of myself. It naturally spilled over onto my relationships with other people, as I had no trouble catching everyone around me doing things wrong all the time. As you can imagine, I was not exactly the most popular guy, and of course there was a lot of friction in my relationships, which made it really hard to get things done and get the support I was hoping for.

When I finally realized what I was doing and learned about the power of catching people doing things right, I made a *conscious decision* to stop being so critical of everybody and started to *actively appreciate* the people in my life. Notice that I had to go through the four stages of competence to install this habit—at first, I didn't know what I was doing (unconscious incompetence); then I became aware of it (conscious incompetence); then I made a conscious decision to change (conscious competence).

I can't honestly say that I'm *unconsciously competent* at Catching People Doing Things Right. The truth is that I was so critical of myself and others for so long that catching people doing things wrong became the habit that was ingrained in my consciousness and behavior patterns.

However, I now find that everything in my life and business runs a lot smoother than it did before—because I consciously make it a daily habit to Catch People Doing Things Right.

EVERYTHING RUNS A LOT SMOOTHER NOW.

Is everyone around me perfect? Do they always do things exactly the way I want? I'm not sure what planet that happens on, but apparently it's not Earth. However, people are far more willing to help me now than they were before, because I've made it a habit to acknowledge and appreciate them.

Another surprising benefit is that the more I started to catch other people doing things right, the more I began to catch myself doing things right. As I appreciated others, I also started to appreciate myself more. So make sure you catch other people doing things right, because some of that appreciation might end up spilling onto you.

HOW TO CATCH PEOPLE DOING THINGS RIGHT

How do you Catch People Doing Things Right? Here are some simple things you can do right now, starting today:

1. Put a Post-it Note on someone's desk saying, "I appreciate what you did."

2. Send them an encouraging email saying, "Great job on that project."

3. Call them and tell them about the difference they've made in your life.

4. Mail them a thank you card.

5. Say to them, "Thank you. I appreciate you."

6. Praise them in front of others.

7. Listen.

There are scores of ways to Catch People Doing Things Right every day of your life, but the most important part of this habit is *your willingness to do it.* Remember that invisible sign everyone is wearing: "Please make me feel important." As you go through your day today, imagine that you can see that invisible sign on every person you meet. This will help you consciously remember to catch the people in your life doing something right every single day.

You'll discover that the more you do this habit, the more you'll WANT to do it, because it feels so good—you'll feel better, the people around you will feel better, and life will simply become a lot happier and more fun. That's why, when you install this Power Habit, you'll win, the people around you will win, and the world will become a better place to live in!

NOAH'S NOTES (IN A NUTSHELL)

1. Many people are stuck because they don't know the Systems of their life or business and because they don't know how to fix these Systems when they're not working properly.

2. The **Five Essential Systems of Support** are: **People, Activities, Environment, Introspection**, and **Simplify**.

3. Your **People System** is the most essential System of Support, and upgrading it the third Power Habit, because human beings run everything on Earth.

4. Start doing **The 5 B.A.S.I.C. People System Habits** described in this chapter so you can enjoy happier, healthier relationships with the people in your life, and start attracting the right people so you can advance your life and career.

5. Start by answering these questions:

   a. To whom can I **Be Accountable** for installing these Power Habits?

   b. From whom can I **Ask for the Support I Need**?

   c. How will I **Seek to Add Value First** in my relationships today?

   d. How can I **Install Fail-Safes** to make sure I stay on track?

   e. How can I **Catch People Doing Things Right** today?

#POWERHABITSCHALLENGE #3

1. For your third Power Habits Challenge, write a post or share a video about why Upgrading Your People System is important, and explain one thing you're going to do from this chapter this week, using the hashtag #PowerHabitsChallenge.

2. Be sure to tag me @NoahStJohn so I'll see your post.

CHAPTER 9

POWER HABIT #4: ACTIVATE YOUR ACTIVITIES SYSTEM

"The time at our disposal each day is elastic; the passions we feel dilate it, those that inspire us shrink it, and habit fills it."
— Marcel Proust

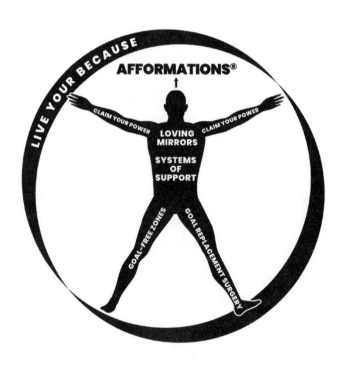

When I coach and mentor busy, hardworking people like you— people who tell me they feel like they have "too much to do and too little time"—I often start by looking at what they're currently doing with the hours and days of their lives.

For example, I was giving my keynote presentation at a real estate conference in New Orleans, and during my keynote, I offered one of my coaching programs called **Power Habits® Academy**. (*Power Habits® Academy* is a six-week coaching program where I teach people how to master The Power Habits® System so you can get rid of your head trash about money in six weeks or less.)

There was a "table rush" of people who wanted to join Power Habits Academy, and one of them was a real estate professional named Brian. Now Brian told me that he'd already invested tens of thousands of dollars in other "mindset" programs—which ended up being "shelf-help"—yet he still felt stuck, overwhelmed, and like he had "too much to do and too little time" (which I will now abbreviate to TMTDATLT).

Do you ever feel like Brian did? If you're like the countless thousands of people I've coached over the last two decades, you might have a similar experience.

That's why I realized that if we want to reach our goals faster, easier, and with less human effort, we need a better way to manage our time. That's why the fourth Power Habit is to **Activate Your Activities System**.

Your *Activities System* is comprised of the Activities you do every day—what you do to fill the hours of each day of your life. While it might sound simplistic, the fact is that we live our lives in days—not in weeks, months, or years.

That's why, if you often find yourself feeling overwhelmed with TMTDATLT, you need to Activate Your Activities System so you can *do less and still get more done*. In short, your Activities System deals with the essential question of "how to increase your personal productivity."

171

A SIMPLE EXERCISE
TO START THIS HABIT

Right now, I'd like you to do this exercise and answer two simple questions. First, take out a piece of paper or use the space below. Draw a vertical line and separate your paper into two columns. Label the left column **"Things I'm Great At"** and the right column **"Things I Suck At."**

Then, fill in both columns: Write the Things You're Great At in the left column and the Things You Suck At in the right column.

For example, my sheet might look like this:

Things I'm Great At	Things I Suck At
✓ Coaching	✓ Self-promotion
✓ Speaking	✓ Cold calling
✓ Writing	
✓ Connecting	

Go ahead and do this simple exercise right now. (I'll wait.)

The fact is, all of us have things we're great at and things we suck at. There are, however, two problems:

1. What if we don't get to do enough of the things we're great at?

2. What if we have to do things we suck at in order to make money?

Rather than asking the questions this way, however, let's flip these around and ask better (more empowering) questions:

1. What do we have to do so we can do more of the things we're great at?

2. What do we have to do in order to complete the tasks we suck at (or don't enjoy) that have to be done in order to make money?

YOUR FOUR PERSONAL RESOURCES

As human beings, we have Four Personal Resources we can use: **Time, Energy, Relationships, and Money**. Out of these, which one is the most valuable?

Some people say that *Energy* is our most valuable personal resource, because everything is made of energy. Your body, your car, your computer, your coffee mug—anything and everything that you and I can see and feel and touch in the physical universe is comprised of energy. Science teaches us that energy is infinite and can be neither created nor destroyed; it just changes form. Therefore, since energy is infinite, it can't be the most valuable human resource.

Others say that *Relationships* are the most important personal resource, because everything we do happens through other human beings. In fact, I just talked about that in the previous chapter. Yet the fact remains that our human relationships often change form and that in order to grow your business or advance your career, you may have to shed certain relationships and invest in others.

What about *Money*? Well, money is just a form of energy. That means that since money is just another form of energy, money itself is also infinite. Of course, *our experience* of money is finite. The way money works is very simple: you have some, and everyone else has all the rest. Therefore, even though most people don't act like it, money isn't the most valuable personal resource either.

The reason that *Time* is the most valuable personal resource is because *it is the only resource that can never be replaced.* **All of Bill Gates's billions**

can't buy one minute of yesterday. Therefore, when I coach people to Activate Their Activities System, I'm really teaching people how to do two things:

1. Doing more of the Activities that ADD to your personal resources of Time, Energy, Relationships, and Money; and

2. Doing fewer of the Activities that TAKE AWAY from your personal resources of Time, Energy, Relationships, and Money.

Now you may be thinking, "But Noah, you just said that I can't get more time since it's the one resource that can never be replaced. So how can I possibly do Activities that give me *more time?*"

I'm glad you asked! (Of course, this is me asking myself, but I hope you're playing along here.)

Yes, the truth is that none of us get more time—because in the game of life, Father Time is undefeated. Yet even if none of us get "more" time, the fact remains that there are *two kinds of time* that we humans can experience—**productive time** and **unproductive time**—and the former creates more space for things we value.

WE DON'T GET MORE TIME. SUCCESS IS DETERMINED BY WHAT WE DO WITH IT.

Productive time means you are doing Activities that are *actively moving you toward your goal* or New Desired Result (the NDR we looked at in an earlier chapter). On the other hand, *unproductive time* means you're either doing Activities that are NOT moving you toward your NDR, or you're doing Activities that are actually *moving you away* from reaching your NDR.

For example, one of your goals might be to lose weight; that's your New Desired Reality you want to reach. Yet you spend your time sitting on the couch eating junk food and watching TV. You're still doing Activities, because eating junk food and watching TV are still *things you do.* But will doing these specific Activities will help you reach your stated goal or NDR? Of course not!

The fact is that no matter what you do, you're still doing SOMETHING. To use our procrastination example, you say you want to grow your business or advance your career—that's your NDR. Yet you spend your time watching cat videos on YouTube and messing around on social media. You're still *doing something*—the clock is still ticking. But are these Activities going to move you toward your New Desired Reality? That would be a no.

That's why one of the realities of this Power Habit is that *time is going to continue to move forward, no matter what you do or don't do.* In the game of life, Father Time is undefeated. (I know I just said that, but it bears repeating.) That's also why the entire field of time management is a misnomer—because we can't actually "manage time." Time just is; we can't manage it. All we can do is *manage our actions and control what we do*—which is why this Power Habit is called Activate Your Activities System.

WHAT YOU'RE DOING THAT'S HOLDING YOU BACK

When people do this next exercise in my live seminars and mastermind groups, they're often amazed to discover just how much of their time they're spending doing unproductive Activities that aren't moving them toward their NDR. Yet in this world of infinite distractions, it's easier than ever to waste time—and harder than ever to use time productively.

First, take out that paper you just filled out with the Things You're Great At and the Things You Suck At. Then, answer the following questions as honestly as you can:

1. What percentage of my week am I currently doing Things I'm Great At?

2. What percentage of my week am I currently doing Things I Suck At?

3. What is one step I can take this week so I can do MORE of the Things I'm Great At?

4. What is one step I can take this week so I can do LESS of the Things I Suck At?

A *resource* is defined as "a stock or supply of assets that can be drawn on by a person or organization in order to function effectively." As we've seen, since time is the most valuable personal resource (because it can never be replaced), and since Father Time is undefeated (yes, I said it again), one of the smartest things we can do is to start doing more of the Things We're Great At (and Enjoy) and less of the Things We Suck At (and Don't Enjoy).

I just added those two additional conditions, because when you start getting clear on What You're Great At (and Enjoy) and What You Suck At (and Don't Enjoy), you can start to make better choices with how you spend your (limited) personal resource of Time.

For example, when Brian, the client I talked about earlier in this chapter, first joined my Power Habits® Academy program, he went through the exercises on Activating Your Activities System. He realized that he was spending far too much of his time doing things he sucked at and didn't enjoy, and hardly any time doing things he was great at and enjoyed. So he started to find ways to do more of what he was great at and enjoyed by taking time away from doing things he sucked at, didn't enjoy, and were moving him away from reaching his own NDR.

I HELPED BRIAN STOP DOING THINGS HE SUCKED AT AND START DOING MORE OF WHAT HE WAS GREAT AT.

Here's a sobering statistic: according to the Bureau of Labor Statistics, the average American spends an average of three hours per day watching television. (Of course, that number varies widely based on age group; for instance, millennials spend less time watching TV than baby boomers and seniors, but far more time on their phones and other portable screens than older generations.)

That adds up to nearly 21 hours per week—or *nearly an entire day every week*—spent watching television. Well, you might say, "But I don't watch TV." Tell you what—just for fun, keep a journal this week and write down every time you turn on the television. Then add up the hours at the end of the week to see how much time this week you actually spent watching TV.

Many of my coaching clients start out by saying to me, "Noah, I want to do such-and-such, but I don't have the time." What if you were to take the time you're currently spending doing mindless, unproductive Activities like watching TV, and replace them with productive Activities like:

- ✓ Writing
- ✓ Reading
- ✓ Learning
- ✓ Getting coaching
- ✓ Being mentored
- ✓ Mentoring
- ✓ Creating content
- ✓ Sharing your message
- ✓ Meditating
- ✓ Getting restful sleep

The truth is, if you desire to have better results in your life, but you keep saying to yourself and others, "I'd love to, but I don't have the time," I want you to realize that *you just told yourself a lie.* That's because whether you choose consciously or unconsciously, in every moment you're making a choice about what you do and how you spend your time. Once time is spent, it can never be taken back. And right now, your choices may be more determined by your head trash that says, "I don't have time" than by your Authentic Self that knows, "I can choose how I spend my time."

BUT WHAT ABOUT MONEY?

Now, the other most popular excuse that people give me as to why they're not doing more of What They're Great At is, "I don't have the money." Have you ever said that to yourself? Have you ever said to yourself or others, "I'd love to do such-and-such, but I just don't have the money"?

Over the last two decades of helping people just like you to add six and seven (and even eight) figures to their businesses while working LESS, I've noticed something funny about human beings—they will make every possible excuse to stay right where they are; yet when it comes to spending money, they will spend it on the craziest things.

For example, remember when Furbies were a thing? How about Cabbage Patch Kids? Snuggies? The Pet Rock, for crying out loud? As I write this, the hottest fad is "weighted blankets." When I was a kid, that was called "put another blanket on."

The point is that all of us have probably fallen victim to buying things we didn't really need while ignoring or neglecting the things we really do. For example, I paid a bunch of "gurus" more than $500,000 to help me grow my business—only to find out that they couldn't teach their way out of a paper bag! Yet because they were very persuasive and great salesmen, they convinced me to part with my hard-earned money; however, they didn't give me any value in return.

The point is that right now, you are spending money on the things that *you decide are important to you*—for example, food, clothing, shelter, and other necessities. However, when you look at your New Desired Reality—your "pot of gold" that you want to get to—ask yourself if you're investing your money in the best possible ways so you can reach your goals faster, easier, and with less human effort.

> THE "GURUS" DON'T GIVE VALUE BECAUSE THEY ALWAYS LEAVE THE GOOD PARTS OUT.

Remember what wise old Benjamin Franklin said: "If a man empties his purse into his head, no man can take it away from him. An investment in knowledge always pays the best interest."

HOW TO DO MORE OF THIS AND LESS OF THAT

Since we've seen that we don't get more time and that all we can do with our time is to spend it as wisely as possible, what's the single best way to do that? Based on my 20-plus years of helping people like you grow their businesses and advance their careers, the crucial step to Activating Your Activities System is to master the skill of **delegating**.

Delegating means "to entrust a task or responsibility to another person." Why is delegating the most important skill if you want to reach your goals faster? Because one person can only do so much, but many people working toward a specific goal means that goal can be reached much faster. As John D. Rockefeller said, "I would rather earn 1 percent of a hundred people's efforts than 100 percent of my own efforts."

ARE YOU DELEGATING THE THINGS YOU SHOULDN'T BE DOING?

For example, everyone knows Sir Richard Branson, founder of Virgin Airlines, as one of the most successful entrepreneurs of the last century. Yet Sir Richard doesn't fly any of the planes. So what does Sir Richard actually do? As far as I can tell, Richard Branson's job is basically to walk around and be charming.

Of course, I'm exaggerating slightly. The fact, however, is that no matter what you think of him, Sir Richard has done a masterful job of creating the public image or persona that he doesn't really work much, and he has a wonderfully talented team of people around him who do the work.

Of course, you and I probably don't own an airline like Sir Richard. Maybe for you, one of the Activities you could start to delegate is as mundane as laundry. Yet keep in mind that if you are doing laundry, that means you are not doing something else. Is there someone else who could do the laundry, so you can do the things that can help you reach your NDR faster?

For example, when Brian, the client to whom I introduced you earlier in this chapter, realized that he was spending too much time doing things he sucked at, he started to delegate those things to others. He told me that what used to take him three to four hours per day now takes him just 15 minutes! Imagine getting all that time back in your life—what would you do with it?

I have found, however, that delegating can be one of the hardest things for entrepreneurs to do, because they say either "I don't have anyone to delegate to" or "I don't trust anyone enough to do things as well as I do them."

This creates a chicken-and-egg situation: you don't have anyone to delegate to, which means your business isn't growing fast enough, which means you don't have the money to hire someone, which means you don't have anyone to delegate to.

So the reality is that at some point, you're simply going to have to bite the bullet and do it. There will never be the "right time" to do this, any more than there's a "right time" to have a baby. You just have to make a decision and do your best, like we all do. I've listed some helpful resources to get you started on delegating at the end of this chapter.

And what happened to Brian? As a result of following my Power Habits® Academy program, not only was he able to gain three to four hours back in his day, he earned $95,000 in sales in just 12 days. That's not a typo.

He also raised $1.2 million for his church so they could build a new addition on the property. That was something he told me he always wanted to do as a way to give back to his community and leave a legacy. He told me that he never thought he'd be able to experience results like that and that his results far exceeded anything he'd ever done in the past.

The fact is, the more you practice Activating Your Activities System, the easier it will become for you. Whether you've never delegated to anyone before, or you have a few people working for you, or you're responsible for a team of hundreds, install this Power Habit so you can go from where you are to where you want to be faster, easier, and with far less effort than ever before!

NOAH'S NOTES (IN A NUTSHELL)

1. If you're feeling overwhelmed or like you have "too much to do and too little time" (TMTDATLT), it's crucial that you make better, more empowered decisions about how you spend your time.

2. That's why Power Habit #4 is **Activate Your Activities System**, because it means starting to make better choices about how and where you spend your personal resources every day.

3. The four personal resources are **Time**, **Energy**, **Relationships**, and **Money**. Those are the only resources we humans have on Earth.

4. The most valuable resource is Time, because it's the only one that can never be replaced. The problem is that most people waste a great deal of Time doing things that aren't moving them toward their New Desired Reality.

5. Answer the questions and do the exercises in this chapter to begin to Activate Your Activities System, so you can reach your New Desired Reality with less time, effort, and money than you're spending right now.

6. Join thousands of people just like you in my online learning academy, **Power Habits® Academy**, at: **www.PowerHabitsAcademy.com**.

#POWERHABITSCHALLENGE #4

1. For your fourth Power Habits Challenge, write a post or share a video about why Activating Your Activities System is important, and explain one thing you're going to do from this chapter this week, using the hashtag #PowerHabitsChallenge.

2. Be sure to tag me @NoahStJohn so I'll see your post.

CHAPTER 10

POWER HABIT #5: ENHANCE YOUR ENVIRONMENT SYSTEM

*"It is a common habit to blame life upon the environment.
Environment modifies life but does not govern life.
The soul is stronger than its surroundings."*
— William James

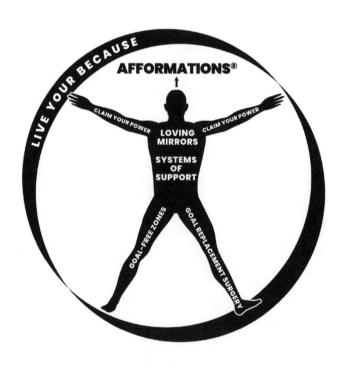

In my keynote speeches, private workshops, and live seminars, I often ask my audience members: "How many people feel that clutter is a problem in your life?" About 80 percent of the hands go up. With all of the organizational tools, calendars, and apps at our disposal, why is clutter still a problem for so many people? For that matter, why is clutter a problem anyway?

One of my coaching clients named Sherrie said to me when we got to this Power Habit that she felt that clutter was a problem in her life. I asked her why she felt that way. She said that her workspace was such a mess that she couldn't even see the carpet in her office. I agreed that yes, that could be a problem!

While your specific issue with clutter may not be as daunting as that, you may still be facing some sort of clutter challenge. That's why the fifth Power Habit is to **Enhance Your Environment System**.

Your *Environment System* consists of the surroundings or conditions in which you live and operate. In short, it's where you live, where you work, and HOW you live and HOW you work, every day of your life.

THE TWO THINGS THAT DETERMINE YOUR QUALITY OF LIFE

As I showed you in an earlier chapter, your success in life is dependent on mastering your Inner Game and your Outer Game. In this Power Habit, we're going to dig even deeper into this understanding by realizing that each of us lives in two environments: our **Inner Environment** and our **Outer Environment**.

Let's start with the Outer Environment, because it's easy to see how this affects our lives. Your *Outer Environment* is the physical environment that you can experience with your five senses: because you can see, hear, smell, taste, and touch it. Your Outer Environment consists of two parts:

your *Home Environment* (where you live) and your *Work Environment* (where you work).

Just as you can experience your Outer Environment with your five senses, your *Inner Environment* is the environment that exists beyond your senses. Just as your Outer Environment is the physical world in which you live, your Inner Environment is the metaphysical world in which you live. And just as you live in two Outer Environments (Home and Work), you also live in two Inner Environments: your *Emotional Environment*—which consists of the emotional state of being you're in at any given moment—and your *Spiritual Environment,* or your connection to something greater than yourself.

Now don't freak out about that word *metaphysical*; it simply means "more than physical." The prefix *meta-* is a Greek word meaning "more than." So, your Outer Environment is the physical world in which you live, the one that's easy to spot because it's right in front of your face.

However, your Inner Environment is the metaphysical or *more-than-physical* world that exists inside of you. The irony is that it is your Inner Environment (your emotions and spirit) that experiences your Outer Environment.

There are only two things that determine your quality of life: the quality of your communication with the world inside of you, and the quality of your communication with the world outside of you. That's because every person lives in two different worlds—we experience our Outer Environment through our five physical senses of sight, hearing, smell, taste, and touch. But who is actually experiencing these things?

The answer is that *you experience your Outer Environment through your Inner Environment.* That's because your Inner Environment consists of your emotions, your mind, and your soul. As scholars, theologians, and philosophers have been telling us for centuries, these are the things that you can't experience through your five senses, but that doesn't mean they're not there.

YOUR FAMILIAR ZONE

Every motivational speaker on the planet says the same thing: that in order to grow, you've got to "get out of your comfort zone." How many times have you heard that one? But consider the following:

Imagine that you're driving down the road of life with one foot on the brake.

Imagine that you're holding yourself back from the success you're capable of.

Imagine that you know you're destined for greater things than you're experiencing right now.

Imagine that you've spent a lot of time, money, and effort on personal or business growth programs, yet you still feel "stuck."

So here's my question to you...

Are any of these feelings "comfortable"?

Is the feeling of driving down the road of life with your foot on the brake *comfortable*?

Is holding yourself back from success *comfortable*?

Is feeling stuck *comfortable*?

Now that I put it to you in that way, you realize that these are not "comfortable" at all. In fact, they are decidedly UNcomfortable!

What they may be, however, is *familiar*.

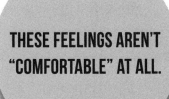

THESE FEELINGS AREN'T "COMFORTABLE" AT ALL.

I want you to look at that word *familiar*. What does that word look like to you? Exactly—*family*. *Family* is the root of the word *familiar*. (One of my coaching clients pointed out that it looks like "family-liar"!)

The point of this exercise is to prove to you that you don't need to "break out of your comfort zone." Do you know why? *Because your "comfort zone" doesn't exist.* The fact is, there's no such thing as a "comfort zone" in the way the motivational speakers told us.

There is, however, a **Familiar Zone.**

What's a Familiar Zone, as opposed to a "comfort zone?" Whereas your comfort zone is a physical and/or metaphysical place where you are, in fact, comfortable, your *Familiar Zone* is the physical and/or metaphysical space that you are accustomed to, is well-known to you, and that you may have been living in for a long, long time.

For instance, you may be very *familiar* with living with clutter—because you've been living that way for so long. Yet it's not entirely *comfortable*, because you know there's a better way to live.

In another example, you may be *familiar* with holding yourself back from the success you're capable of. You may be *familiar* with not getting the results you desire. You may be *familiar* with driving down the road of life with one foot on the brake. Yet you're probably not very *comfortable* with these things.

That's why the one of the main purposes of The Power Habits® System is to empower you to **Expand Your Familiar Zone.**

Notice that I didn't say to "get out of your familiar zone." That wouldn't make any sense, because when you "get out" of something, it means you're not in it anymore. Yet we all need the feelings of familiarity in our lives and at work in order to thrive.

WHEN YOU USE MY POWER HABITS® SYSTEM, YOU WILL EXPAND YOUR FAMILIAR ZONE.

So, one of the wonderful benefits of installing my Power Habits® System is that you will automatically Expand Your Familiar Zone—meaning that, over time, you will grow more familiar with things like more success, greater happiness, and personal fulfillment—things you may not be as familiar with right now.

HOW TO CLEAR YOUR OUTER CLUTTER

If I ever decide to retire from the business and personal growth industry and start another business, it will probably be in the self-storage industry. Why? Because Americans are obsessed with buying more and more stuff. And when there's too much stuff in the house, do they get rid of any of it? No, they put the car outside and put more stuff in the garage. Then, when the garage is full, do they get rid of stuff? No, they buy a storage unit to store their stuff. Then when that storage unit is full, do they get rid of stuff? No, they get another storage unit. (Right now, you are probably either laughing because this hits too close to home, or not laughing because this hits too close to home.)

The point is, many of my coaching clients and mastermind students have faced this insidious problem of having too much stuff and not being able to let go of it. Going back to the questions that opened this chapter, why do so many people still have a problem with clutter, and why is it a problem anyway? Isn't the purpose of life to gather "more stuff"—like the famous saying, "He who dies with the most toys wins?"

> "HE WHO DIES WITH THE MOST TOYS WINS." REALLY?

The fact is, we all want to have nice things. And it's true that some people value possessions (things) more than others. For example, I haven't worn a watch in more than 30 years, because I don't like wearing watches. To me, they feel uncomfortable and I can always look at my phone or ask someone if I need to know what time it is. For those reasons, I don't own a single watch, because I couldn't care less about them. On the scale of 1 to 10 on the "must have watch" department, I'd score a minus 20.

However, lots of people like watches and spend a lot of money on cool-looking watches. In addition, many people wear expensive (or expensive-looking) watches as status symbols—i.e., "Look at this expensive watch I'm wearing; I must be successful." Heck, even I agree that some watches do make the wearer look successful.

In short, there's a lot of truth to the saying, "One person's trash is another person's treasure." I couldn't care less about watches, while some people get very excited about them. Who's right and who's wrong? No one. Yet I would argue that one of the reasons I'm able to keep my Home and Work Environment relatively clutter-free is because I simply don't care all that much about "gathering more stuff."

There are thousands of books, tools, and apps to help you get organized and clear the clutter. Yet what I've noticed with many of my coaching clients is that even though they know these tools exist, they're not using them.

Therefore, if you'd like to finally clear the clutter from your Outer Environment (Home and/or Work), I encourage you to answer the following questions:

1. What clutter am I facing in my Home Environment?

2. What clutter am I facing in my Work Environment?

3. What benefit do I get from holding on to this clutter?

4. How would it benefit me to clear the clutter from my Home Environment?

5. How would it benefit me to clear the clutter from my Work Environment?

Have you ever noticed that when you clear the clutter from your home or work, you feel better? Based on my experience coaching and mentoring countless thousands of people just like you, I'll bet you've had this experience many times. Therefore, when you clear the clutter in your Outer Environment on a consistent basis, you'll be giving yourself a gift that will keep on giving.

HOW TO CLEAR YOUR INNER CLUTTER

Now that we've begun to tackle your Outer Environment, let's turn to your Inner Environment. It's easy to spot clutter in your Outer Environment, because it's right in front of your face: that pile of mail, those unanswered emails, those filing cabinets that haven't been organized since the Reagan Administration. But how do we spot clutter in our Inner Environment, when we can't see it in the first place?

Remember that your Inner Environment is comprised of your Emotional Environment and your Spiritual Environment. In the Emotional Environment, the two biggest blocks for most people are **resentment** and **fear**. *Resentment* is emotional clutter about the past; *fear* is emotional clutter about the future.

For example, let's say you've been hurt or injured by people in your past (and who among us can say we haven't?). However, let's say that, even though these injuries happened long ago, you're still carrying them with you, and those hurts are forming your habits today—even though the cause of them may have happened years or even decades ago.

If this is the case, you may be holding on to the emotional block called *resentment*, which is defined as "bitter indignation at being

ARE YOU STILL HOLDING ON TO HURTS FROM YEARS OR DECADES AGO?

treated unfairly." Doesn't that definition fit so perfectly—and notice that the word *bitter* is a sensory word we can literally taste!

Resentment is always about the past, because it's impossible to feel resentment about something that hasn't happened yet. We can, however, feel the emotion of *fear* when it comes to the future. In fact, the future is all we CAN fear—because we can't fear the past (since it already happened) and we can't fear the present, because we're living in it right now. For instance, if you're on a plane and you're afraid of being in a plane crash, you're still fearing the future, because you're imagining something that hasn't happened yet.

Therefore, the dual emotions of resentment (emotional clutter about the past) and fear (emotional clutter about the future) are the two biggest blocks in most people's Emotional Environment.

In terms of your Spiritual Environment, many people's biggest spiritual block is that *they don't believe miracles can happen for them.* For example, many people mistakenly believe things like, "I've done too many dumb things in my life and made too many mistakes, so it's probably too late for me."

One example of this is that after my keynote speeches or at my live seminars, people will come up to me and tell me that they've lost their connection to God or something greater than themselves, because they've lost someone or something very close to them.

The fact is that if you're old enough to read this book, you've probably lost someone or something that meant a lot to you. However, just because you've lost someone or something very dear to you does NOT mean that God has abandoned you. In fact, what happens when we face a loss is that *we abandon God.*

We human beings experience *gain* and *loss* all the time throughout our lives—and of course, we like to "gain" a lot more than we like to "lose." This is why, when we gain, we say, "Thank you, God!" but when we lose, we say, "God, how could you do this to me?"

I want you to begin to believe that *miracles can happen for you too*—and not just for other people. I also want you to realize that not only can miracles happen for you, but *you are a miracle.*

MIRACLES CAN HAPPEN FOR YOU TOO.

For instance, think about the other planets in our solar system, the stars in our galaxy, the universe itself—nowhere else that we know of is there life, let alone human life, let alone all the natural beauty of our fragile planet Earth.

When you look at it this way, isn't it amazing what a miracle life itself is? That's why every one of us has to work very hard right now to protect the environment of our planet—because it's the only home we've got. Just as we have to clear the clutter in our individual lives, if we want to continue to live on this planet, we're going to have to figure out how to clear the clutter from the planet itself.

HOW TO MAKE THIS A HABIT

Let's return to our Habit Loop so we can start to make Enhancing Our Environment System one of our daily habits.

First, we have the *Cue.* In the case of your Environment System, let's say something comes into your Outer Environment. Perhaps you receive an email (or 50), or maybe someone hands you a physical document like snail mail. Let's call that "thing" the *input*—the thing that comes into your environment that you have to deal with, one way or the other.

The next question is: What do you do with this input? For example, do you let things pile up until they become unmanageable? Do you ignore them until the pile becomes overwhelming and you have no

WE DON'T LIVE IN THE INFORMATION AGE. WE LIVE IN THE INFORMATION OVERLOAD AGE.

choice but to deal with it? What is your current *Routine?*

If you are someone who is *familiar* with living in a state of environmental clutter, you probably don't have a very good system for dealing with the inputs that come into your life every day. One of the big problems, however, is that we don't live in the Information Age; we live in **the Information Overload Age**.

According to Google CEO Eric Schmidt, every 48 hours human beings create as much information as *all of humanity did* from the dawn of civilization until the year 2003. That is approximately five exabytes of data produced every 48 hours.

By way of comparison, a megabyte is a thousand kilobytes or the equivalent of a small book. A gigabyte is a thousand megabytes or about ten yards of books on a shelf. An exabyte is approximately one billion gigabytes, which is equivalent to *all of the words ever spoken by mankind.*

So, let me repeat: the human race today creates as much information every 48 hours as was created from the dawn of man through the year 2003. That is a staggering and literally overwhelming number.

One question I sometimes ask at my keynote speeches is: "How many of you think that the crush of information will start to lessen in the next five years?" Naturally, no one raises their hand. We all know that it's only going to get worse and worse as time goes on. That's why it's more important than ever to master this Power Habit.

Okay, you've identified your Cue—an input comes in—and now you know your current Routine (you ignore it, let things pile up, get upset, etc.). So now I want you to create a new Routine based on what I've shown you in this chapter.

Remember Sherrie, my coaching client I introduced you to earlier in this chapter? She told me that her workspace was so cluttered that she couldn't even see the carpet in her office. After I worked with her on this Power Habit, she realized that holding on to clutter in her Work Environment was not just costing her time, it was also costing her a lot of money and opportunity.

So she installed a Routine called "I take care of inputs immediately." She began to systematically clear the clutter from her office that had been accumulating for years. She told me that it took *17 garbage bags* to clear all the clutter from her workspace. No wonder she hadn't been able to see the carpet!

But guess what? She immediately felt better and more empowered. She began feeling more confident talking with people. In less than 90 days after clearing the clutter from her workspace, Sherrie had made enough extra money in her business that she was able to *replace the carpet that she hadn't even been able to see before working with me.*

Another one of my clients did this exercise, cleared the clutter from her office, and found $150 worth of gift cards that she had lost two years earlier. Wouldn't it be nice to get paid to clean your office? The point is—and I know you've experienced this for yourself—whenever you give yourself the gift of clearing the clutter, you make space for more good things—things like money, peace of mind, opportunity—to come in.

Then, I want you to identify the Reward you'll get when you clear the clutter from your environment. Maybe it's a sense of accomplishment. Maybe it's a feeling of success, achievement, or completion. Maybe it's the knowledge that you're finally in charge of your life and won't be controlled by clutter anymore. Whatever it is, I want you to make it a powerful Reward for you and your brain to latch on to.

SHE MADE ENOUGH MONEY TO REPLACE THE CARPET SHE HADN'T EVEN BEEN ABLE TO SEE BEFORE!

Finally, use Afformations® to install new Beliefs. For example, you could Afform...

Why is it so easy for me to keep my workspace clean?

Why do I love being organized?

Why do I enjoy clearing the clutter and being clutter-free?

IF YOU'RE STUCK, START HERE

Over the years, many coaching clients have asked me, "Noah, if I want to get unstuck and get organized, should I start with my Inner Environment or my Outer Environment?" It's a logical question, because, as I mentioned earlier in this chapter, we experience our Outer Environment through our Inner Environment, so it makes sense that some people might want to clear their Inner (Emotional and/or Spiritual) clutter first.

However, I always tell my clients the same thing: "Start with your Outer Environment first." Why? Well, in case you haven't noticed, your Outer Environment greatly influences your emotional well-being. For example, if you can't find your papers and you're tripping over stuff in your home or office, it's frustrating, right?

Well, to be *frustrated* is an emotion, and emotions are caused by something else—and frequently, that "something else" is something in our Outer (Home or Work) Environment. Therefore, when you remove the cause of the emotion—in this case, you clear the clutter—you will, in fact, feel better.

So, begin to Enhance Your Environment System by first cleaning out something in your Outer Environment—for example, your

> WHEN YOU MAKE IT A HABIT TO CLEAR THE INNER AND OUTER CLUTTER, YOU'LL FEEL BETTER.

closet, desk, inbox, or anywhere else there's clutter in your Home or Work Environment.

Then, as new inputs come in every day (as they surely will), stick with your new Routine of dealing with those inputs immediately and keeping both of your Environments—Inner and Outer—free from clutter. Making this a habit will pay big dividends for you immediately and in the long run.

One final thought about Enhancing Your Environment System: your Environments are not static and unchanging. They are vibrant, dynamic, and in a constant state of change. That's why, as you find yourself becoming more and more successful, you may need some additional help from others to support you. Because it's so important to your long-term success, we'll be examining this phenomenon throughout this book.

NOAH'S NOTES (IN A NUTSHELL)

1. If you have a problem with clutter, it's time to make healthier, more empowered decisions about how you deal with the inputs in your life and business.

2. That's why Power Habit #5 is **Enhance Your Environment System**, because it means you'll start making better choices about how you deal with the crush of information and "stuff" you have to deal with every day.

3. You live in two major Environments: your **Inner Environment** and your **Outer Environment**.

4. Your Outer Environment consists of your *Home Environment* (where you live) and your *Work Environment* (where you work). Your Inner Environment consists of your *Emotional Environment* (your beliefs and feelings) and your *Spiritual*

Environment (your connection to something greater than yourself).

5. We don't live in the Information Age; we live in the Information Overload Age. That's why it's crucial to Enhance Your Environment System—so you can deal with the crush of information that's coming at us every day and will only continue to get worse in the future.

#POWERHABITSCHALLENGE #5

1. For your fifth Power Habits Challenge, write a post or share a video about why Enhancing Your Environment System is crucial to your success, and describe one thing you're going to do from this chapter this week, using the hashtag #PowerHabitsChallenge.

2. Be sure to tag me @NoahStJohn so I'll see your post.

CHAPTER 11

POWER HABIT #6: INSTALL YOUR INTROSPECTION SYSTEM

"Character is simply habit long continued."
— Plutarch

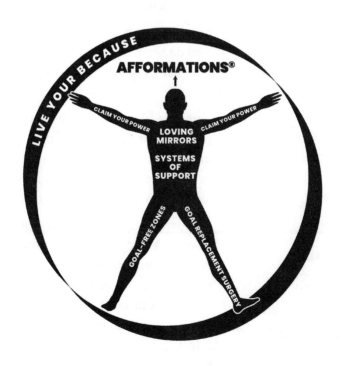

Imagine that you're in the middle of a typical workday—answering emails, making phone calls, writing reports, and so forth. Suddenly your phone rings. You answer the phone and a family member tells you that someone very close to you was just involved in an accident and is in the emergency room.

What do you say in that moment?

Do you say, "Sorry, I'm too busy"?

Do you say, "I'll get around to it later"?

Do you say, "This wasn't on my schedule today; how about next week?"

Of course not.

What you do is, you hang up the phone, drop everything, tell your co-workers what happened, and rush to the ER.

Now, it's clear that "Go to hospital" was NOT on your to-do list today. This was not a meeting you had on your calendar. Yet what happened what you got that phone call? What happened was your PRIORITIES got switched up in an instant.

Most of us have had experiences like this—because "emergencies" are not something you can put on your schedule. (If they were, we'd call them "planneds.") The point is that when emergencies such as this happen, your schedule goes out the window, because your true priorities are revealed in that moment.

YOUR VALUES AND PRIORITIES ARE REVEALED THROUGH YOUR DAILY HABITS.

This is why the sixth Power Habit is called **Install Your Introspection System**. Because your true priorities and core values get revealed in emergencies, you don't want to wait until an emergency happens in order to live them. In short, you need to Install Your Introspection System so you can reveal your true priorities and core values *each and every day.*

WHY INTROSPECTION IS CRUCIAL TO YOUR SUCCESS

To *introspect* literally means "to look within." I talked in an earlier chapter about the fact that we live in two worlds: the world outside of us and the world inside of us. That is why the quality of your life is dependent on just two things: the quality of your communication with the world *outside* of you and the quality of your communication with the world *inside* of you.

Let me give you an example. On October 3, 1945, a ten-year-old boy stood onstage at the Mississippi-Alabama Fair and Dairy Show talent contest. He was dressed as a cowboy. One of his teachers had encouraged him to enter the contest after hearing him sing during morning prayers. He had to stand on a chair to reach the microphone. He placed fifth.

A few months later, he received a guitar for his eleventh birthday. (What he really wanted was a rifle or a bicycle.) Two of his uncles and the new pastor at the family church gave him basic guitar lessons. He learned mostly by watching other people.

But he didn't like singing in public. He was too shy.

In 1948, his family moved from Tupelo, Mississippi, to Memphis, Tennessee. The boy would spend every moment of his free time on Beale Street, the heart of the Memphis blues scene. He'd often bring his guitar to school.

Yet his eighth grade teacher gave him a C in music. She told him that he had "no gift for singing."

During his teenage years, he was often bullied by classmates and called a "mama's boy." Still painfully shy, he nevertheless stood out because of his appearance—including long sideburns, slicked-back hair, and funky clothes.

In 1953, the young man walked into the offices of Sun Records to create his first record. The receptionist asked him whom he sounded like. The young man replied, "I don't sound like nobody."

But the record went nowhere. He tried out for a local singing group but failed the audition. He told his father, "They told me I couldn't sing."

Unbeknownst to the young man, Sam Phillips, owner of Sun Records, had been saying to his friends, "If I could find a white man who had the Negro sound and the Negro feel, I could make a billion dollars."

THEY TOLD HIM HE COULDN'T SING.

Then Sam heard this young man's record. Sam invited him back to the studio and asked him to sing as many songs as he knew. Yet even then, the recording session was not going well.

The young man and his backup musicians were about to pack it up and go home, when the young man suddenly picked up his guitar and started signing a 1946 blues song, "That's All Right."

In the words of one of the musicians from that legendary session:

"All of a sudden, [he] just started singing this song, jumping around and acting the fool, and then Bill picked up his bass, and he started acting the fool, too, and I started playing with them.

"Sam, I think, had the door to the control booth open…he stuck his head out and said, 'What are you doing?' And we said, 'We don't know.' 'Well, back up,' Sam said, 'try to find a place to start, and do it again.'"

Phillips immediately began taping; he knew this was the sound he'd been looking for. Sun Records released the album. No one had ever heard anything like it before.

And within three years, Elvis Presley was an international superstar—the most famous human being on the planet.

Several years ago, I gave a private workshop for a company based near Memphis and was taken on a private tour of Graceland, Elvis's Memphis mansion and now a National Historic Landmark.

Elvis died on August 16, 1977, so his home is decorated in that distinctive 1970s style and will remain that way forever. One thing that surprised me, however, is that Graceland is much smaller than you might imagine. For example, the kitchen is positively cramped. The pool in the backyard—the one you see in all those Elvis home movies—is only average size.

The undisputed showpiece of Graceland is the enormous display of his different costumes, shimmering sequins and bursting with color. Yet when you visit the small garden in the back of the house where Elvis, his mother, and stillborn brother are buried, it's impossible not to stand in awe and humility.

Elvis Presley was the world's first modern superstar. He transcended race, age, and even death, as his estate continues to make more money every year after his death than Elvis ever made while he was alive.

Of course, the tragedy of Elvis Presley's story is that he died at the age of 42, and the circumstances leading up to his death remain shrouded in mystery. Yet what is clear is that for most of his career, Elvis was controlled by "Colonel Tom" Parker (born Andreas Cornelis van Kuijk), a man who cared more about making profits for himself than caring for his one and only client.

Would we have lost Elvis so young if he had installed this habit of Introspection? Might he have realized sooner that he didn't have to churn out one low-budget studio movie after another and instead used his unique talents for something greater? Might he have been able to kick the binge-eating and prescription drug habits that ultimately led to his early demise?

WHAT IF ELVIS PRESLEY HAD INSTALLED THIS HABIT OF INTROSPECTION?

And what about all the other gifted people who died far too young due to problems with drugs, alcohol, or other addictions? Robin Williams. Andy Gibb. Chris Farley. Heath Ledger. John Belushi. Philip Seymour Hoffman. Amy Winehouse. Marilyn Monroe. What if they and others like them had had access to this information—would things have turned out differently?

That's why Installing Your Introspection System is not just crucial to your success; it's also crucial to your life. Of course, it's easy to see clearly in hindsight. Yet the fact remains that if you don't Install your Introspection System, the crush of Information Overload can overwhelm even the most peaceful among us.

In *The 7 Habits of Highly Effective People*, Stephen Covey writes about the fact that we need to make sure that our "ladder of success is leaning against the right wall." But how exactly should we do that?

THE SURPRISING BENEFITS OF INTROSPECTION

As we've already seen, the world is a noisy place, and it's only getting noisier. Yet whenever you take a walk in nature, go to the beach, or even just look up at the sky, have you ever noticed that you instantly feel better? Why does this happen?

This happens because when you walk in nature or even just look up at the sky, it immediately triggers your Introspection System. For example, a recent study from the Nippon Medical School in Tokyo found that "forest bathing"—what the Japanese call *Shinrin-yoku*—has remarkable, measurable health benefits. A simple walk in nature can help you reduce stress, fight depression, lower blood pressure, and may even help prevent cancer.

Yet you didn't need a scientific study to tell you what you already knew—that when you perform an introspective exercise like walking in nature, you immediately feel better. The main reason to Install Your Introspection System is not just for the obvious health benefits that come from fresh air and exercise; the main reason is because you want to make sure that the path you're currently on is the one you actually want to be on.

A SIMPLE WALK IN NATURE WILL GIVE YOU MEASURABLE HEALTH BENEFITS.

Going back to an analogy I used earlier in this book, imagine that you wanted to drive from Los Angeles to New York. Would you just jump in your car, start driving around, and hope that you would somehow reach your desired destination? Of course not!

Before you even got on the road, you'd make sure you had a basic understanding of where you were going. When you got on the road, you'd constantly be checking your GPS to make sure you're going in the right direction. And you'd make any necessary course corrections along the way.

The problem is, many people are living their lives without checking in with themselves and seeing if they are, in fact, traveling on the right road to success. Like Elvis Presley, many people are so swamped with just the fact of living day to day that they forget or neglect to check in with themselves to see if where they're going is where they actually want to go. (We'll talk more about this phenomenon in the chapter on Goal Replacement Surgery.)

HOW TO INSTALL YOUR INTROSPECTION SYSTEM

Let's return to our Habit Loop so we can begin to install this Power Habit. First, identify the Cue. For example, right now, when you wake up in the morning, your normal routine might be to worry about all the

WHAT IF YOU REPLACED YOUR ROUTINE OF WORRY WITH ONE OF GRATITUDE?

five million things you have to do that day. But is that really the most productive thing to do with your time? Probably not.

So, let's install a new habit—one that will empower you to get far better results with less time and effort.

We start with the Cue—in this case, you wake up.

Then we go to the Routine. Right now, your Routine could be called "worry." But what if we replaced that with a more empowering Routine—something that could actually benefit you instead of sap your energy?

For example, when you wake up in the morning, you could do any or all of the following:

✓ Meditate

✓ Pray

✓ Write in your Power Habits Journal

✓ Thank God for the gifts of your life

✓ Visualize things going well today

✓ Listen to iAfform® Audios

✓ Write your new Afformations

Now some will argue: "But Noah, I don't have time for all this!"

Really? You have time to worry, but not to be grateful? You have time to imagine things going badly but not enough time to imagine things going well?

The point is, you're already using your time to imagine the worst. What if you simply replaced that old, disempowering Routine with a new, empowering Routine? It's the same amount of time, but I'll bet the results will be vastly different.

What's your Reward for doing your new Routine? These could include:

- ✓ Peace of mind
- ✓ Reduced stress
- ✓ Lower blood pressure
- ✓ Happier relationships
- ✓ Less bitterness and anger

Nah, you wouldn't want any of those, right? (A little Reward humor, there.)

Over time, you'll start to develop a Craving for that good, peaceful, empowered, healthy feeling, because both you and your brain like to feel good.

And finally, write your new Beliefs in the form of Afformations®. For example:

- ✓ *Why do I love to meditate every morning?*
- ✓ *Why am I so lucky?*
- ✓ *Why am I so grateful for the gifts of my life?*
- ✓ *Why did everything go so well for me today?*

(For more than 400 additional Afformations® on this and many other subjects, visit **www.Afformations.com** and **www.AfformationsBook.com**.)

Yes, I know you're busy, and I know you've got a million and one things to do today. But what makes you think that NOT Installing Your Introspection System will make your day and your life any easier?

UNCONSCIOUSLY SUCCESSFUL PEOPLE DO THESE POWER HABITS® WITHOUT EVEN REALIZING IT.

Over the last two decades of helping people like you make millions of dollars while working less, I've come to realize that **Unconsciously Successful People** (USPs), no matter how busy they are, have installed this habit of Introspection. That's because USPs realize that no matter how many things they have to do today, if they don't practice the habit of Introspection, they've set themselves up for failure.

USPs have developed a set of habits that I call The Power Habits® of Unconsciously Successful People, to ensure that, not only are they doing the right things; they're doing them for the right reasons to keep them going in the right direction—so they can make corrections if they get off track.

And if they can do it, you can do it too.

One final thought about Installing Your Introspection System: Remember the last time you had a hunch that turned out to be right? And remember how many times you did something and then looked back after it was done and said, "Ah man, I *knew* I shouldn't have done that!"

We've all done this. That's one more reason to develop the habit of Installing Your Introspection System—because doing so will strengthen your connection to your intuition or Authentic Self. This will empower you to make better choices in the moment of decision. That's just one of the many benefits of Installing Your Introspection System.

NOAH'S NOTES (IN A NUTSHELL)

1. We live in a world of infinite distractions. The world is a noisy place and is getting noisier.

2. That's why Power Habit #5 is **Install Your Introspection System**—because it means checking in with your Authentic Self to ensure that you are going after the goals you really want and living the life you choose.

3. *Introspection* means "to look within," yet our noisy, distracted world is constantly pulling at us to look outside ourselves for answers.

4. Installing Your Introspection System means doing daily habits to check in with your Authentic Self, your intuition, or the "still, small voice" within.

5. These habits can include doing daily activities like:

   a. Meditation

   b. Prayer

   c. Writing in your Power Habits Journal

   d. Thanking God for the gifts of your life

   e. Visualizing things going well today

   f. Listening to iAfform® Audios (get a free sample and complete your iAfform Audio collection at **www.iAfform.com**)

   g. Writing your new Afformations®

6. Because of Information Overload, daily Introspection is crucial and will only grow more important—and more difficult—as time goes on.

#POWERHABITSCHALLENGE #6

1. For your sixth Power Habits Challenge, write a post or share a video about why Installing Your Introspection System is crucial to your success, and describe one thing you're going to do from this chapter this week, using the hashtag #PowerHabitsChallenge.

2. Be sure to tag me @NoahStJohn so I'll see your post.

CHAPTER 12

POWER HABIT #7: EMBRACE YOUR SIMPLIFY SYSTEM

"We are what we repeatedly do. Excellence, then,
is not an act, but a habit."
— Will Durant

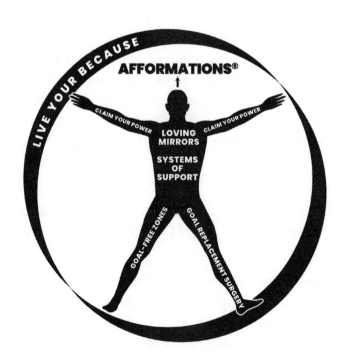

Have you ever thought to yourself, "Boy, I wish things could be more complicated! I wish I had more stuff to do every day!" Unless you enjoy being tortured on a regular basis, it's unlikely that you've ever had, or ever will have, these thoughts.

That's why, when we look at the four preceding Systems of Support that I've laid out for you—your People, Activities, Environment, and Introspection Systems—they lead to just one natural, logical conclusion: *the overarching need to simplify.*

That's why the final System of Support, and what I believe is one of the crowning achievements of The Power Habits® System itself, is **The Simplify System**. And that means the seventh Power Habit is **Embrace Your Simplify System**.

As stated earlier, we don't live in the Information Age; we live in the Information Overload Age. That means that there is simply too much information for any of us to process—too many channels, too many emails, too many websites, too many distractions, too many interruptions. One of the big problems with Information Overload is "paralysis by analysis"—the habit of over-analyzing (or over-thinking) a situation to the point that you never make a decision or take an action because you're afraid of doing the "wrong" thing. Yet that is the very thing that's holding millions of people back from reaching their full potential.

KNOWLEDGE IS (NO LONGER) POWER

There's an ancient phrase we all know that says "Knowledge is power." This phrase originated thousands of years ago when knowledge (or information) was held by the very few: the lords and people in power, who of course didn't like sharing that knowledge with the people over whom they ruled.

Therefore, for 99.9 percent of human history, the phrase "Knowledge is power" was very true. Today, however, the exact reverse has happened—so-called "knowledge" (or information) today is held by, essentially, everyone—any human who has access to the Internet. The Internet is, of course, the greatest communication tool in the history of humanity. The best thing about the Internet is that you can find all the information you want about anything you want. The worst thing about the Internet is that you can find all the information you want about anything you want.

For millions of people, this has resulted in paralysis by analysis, because they simply don't know what they should and shouldn't be doing. That's why in today's Information Overload Age, "knowledge" is no longer power. The true power today is Implementation: the actual act of *getting things done.*

KNOWLEDGE IS NO LONGER POWER. THE TRUE POWER TODAY IS IMPLEMENTATION.

In his 1970 book *Future Shock*, Alvin Toffler introduced the term "overchoice" or "choice overload" where people have a hard time making a decision when faced with too many choices or options. This phenomenon has recently become known as FOMO, or "fear of missing out."

For example, right now you are reading a book that I wrote. I spent countless hours not just writing this book you're reading, but also writing the dozen other books that I've published prior to this one. Each time, for each book, I spent more hours than I could count researching, writing, and rewriting, in order to make every word, every paragraph, every chapter, and every book as valuable to you, the reader, as possible.

If you were to add up the hundreds of thousands of words I've published in my books, articles, and blog posts, and the millions of words I've spoken in my keynote speeches, private workshops, and live seminars over the last 20-plus years, it would come to far more than the 10,000 hours we often hear it takes to achieve mastery.

I MISSED OUT ON A LOT OF THINGS, BECAUSE I HAD A LARGER PURPOSE.

Yet in doing so, I've missed out on a lot of things. I missed out on going to parties. I missed out on spending time with my family. I missed out on traveling and going on vacations. So why did I make those choices instead of doing those other things?

Because I felt that I had a larger purpose. I'll talk more about that in the chapter on Living Your Because, but for now I hope you're starting to see how all of these Power Habits are related.

The point is, when you make a choice to do one thing, it means, by definition, that you aren't doing something else. You can write a book, or you can watch TV. You can call that prospect, or you can watch cat videos on YouTube. The question of, "What should I be doing right now?" may be one of the most (if not *the* most) confusing and confounding questions of our time—for the simple reason that we now have more choices than ever before in human history of how to answer that question.

That's why I want you to write the following sentence in huge letters and place it in your home or office so you'll see it every day: **Simplify your life and streamline your business.**

CONFRONTING BOTTLENECKS

When we start to install this Power Habit of Embrace Your Simplify System with my high-level coaching clients, I encourage them to start with their **bottlenecks**. A *bottleneck* is defined as "someone or something that slows or stops free movement and progress."

Imagine that you're driving on the highway, going (ahem) the speed limit, listening to your favorite tunes, and, of course, singing along at the top of your lungs. (My personal favorites are Journey and Bon Jovi for this particular exercise.) Suddenly, you notice that the traffic ahead of you is slowing down; you see brake lights, so you slow down too. Traffic slows to a crawl, and after what seems an eternity, you finally get to the other side, where you see—nothing at all.

SIMPLIFY YOUR LIFE AND STREAMLINE YOUR BUSINESS.

How many times has this happened to you—where you're forced to slow down or even stop, and then you have no idea why or what happened to cause the slowdown? This is known as *the bottleneck effect*; because just like liquid flows through a bottle very quickly, when it comes to the neck of the bottle, because the space is constricted, it flows far more slowly.

Now this may be fine when you're pouring a drink, because otherwise it might spill all over the place. Yet when it comes to your business, your career, or even your life, the presence of bottlenecks is often the difference between success and failure.

There are three aspects to consider when confronting your business or personal bottlenecks: *Identification, Significance,* and *Cost.* Therefore, do this simple exercise to confront the bottlenecks you may be facing right now. For this example, we're going to use a business—e.g., a business you own—because it's easy for illustrative purposes. Of course, feel free to use these questions in any area where you feel stuck or would like better results.

REMOVING BOTTLENECKS IS THE #1 JOB OF ANY LEADER.

Part 1: Identification

1. What are the current bottlenecks in my business?

2. What is currently stopping my business from growing?

3. Why aren't I getting the results I want?

4. Was there a time when these bottlenecks weren't here?

Part 2: Significance

1. How serious is this problem?

2. Can I remove these bottlenecks myself, with my current knowledge and experience?

3. Would it benefit me to bring in someone to help me remove these bottlenecks?

Part 3: Cost

1. How much money will it cost me this year if I *don't* remove these bottlenecks?

2. How much will it cost me in lost time?

3. What about lost opportunity?

4. What will happen if I don't do anything to remove these bottlenecks in the next 12 months?

WHICH STAGE ARE YOU IN?

After helping countless entrepreneurs and organizations collectively add more than $2.2 billion in sales over the last 20-plus years, I've come to realize that most businesses are in one of four growth stages:

Stage 1: Zero to six figures

Stage 2: Six to seven figures

Stage 3: Seven to eight figures

Stage 4: Eight figures and above

One of the tricks, however, is that *your bottlenecks are different at each stage.* For instance, when you're going from zero (startup) to six figures, you're facing one set of problems or bottlenecks that can slow your growth. Examples of this might be:

✓ Hiring your first employee (or independent contractor)

✓ Deciding where your workspace is

✓ Determining what you (the owner) should be doing and not doing

✓ Dealing with a lack of sales

Then, when you finally hit that elusive six-figure mark, your next set of challenges or bottlenecks to reach the seven-figure mark can include…

✓ Hiring a VP of marketing

✓ Deciding if you should open a second location

✓ Determining what you (the owner) should be doing and not doing

✓ Scaling your operation

And so on, all the way from seven to eight figures and beyond, including how and when you want to exit the business.

IMPLEMENTING WIN CUBED

Whether you're trying to get to your first $10K in sales, you want to get to $100K a year, or you're ready to make your first (or next) million and beyond, I always encourage my coaching clients to implement something we at SuccessClinic.com call **Win Cubed**. You're familiar with the concept of Win-Win, which means "I win and you win," or mutual benefit.

While that's an important principle in human relationships, there's another, even higher level of benefit, which I call a *Win Cubed*. That means Win times Win times Win, or Win to the third power. Win Cubed means "I win, you win, and the world wins."

The fact is that most USPs don't simply focus on their own win and the other person's win; they also focus on the win for the whole world.

Let me give you a personal example from my own business. Years ago, when my books started to sell and I began to get booked on more stages, I started to get more emails. A lot more emails. Then A LOT more emails. Soon, I found more than half of my workday being consumed by responding to every one of the hundreds of emails that were coming in every single day.

UNCONSCIOUSLY SUCCESSFUL PEOPLE FOCUS ON WIN CUBED.

It became obvious that my business simply couldn't grow if I was the one writing the books, giving the keynote presentations, and also answering every email. So email became my #1 bottleneck that I knew I had to confront and eliminate if I wanted to reach the next level so I could help more people.

While I knew that email was the most important daily activity I had to delegate, there was just one teensy problem: there wasn't anyone to delegate to. So I went through this simple exercise to begin to Embrace My Simplify System:

First, I identified the bottlenecks in my business. Then, I chose the bottleneck I wanted to eliminate first. In this case, responding to emails.

MOST PEOPLE WILL DO MORE FOR MEANING THAN FOR MONEY.

Then, I wrote what would be my Win if I were to successfully delegate this task. In this example, I would have more time to devote to things that brought in money, like coaching and doing keynote speeches and live seminars.

Then, I identified the Win for the other person (remember, I hadn't yet identified that person). I realized that she would receive a good salary and would therefore have a nice monetary win. Second, since I would be freed from all that email, I would genuinely appreciate her. I remembered that most people will do more for appreciation than for money, although in this case she'd get both.

Then, I identified what I call the larger Win, or the World Win. I know that might sound dramatic, but the fact is that many people (I argue, most people) will do far more when they know their work contributes to something greater—a larger purpose than just "making money." If you don't believe me, ask yourself this question:

Would I rather make $150,000 a year doing work that I know doesn't contribute to a larger purpose or make $100,000 a year doing work that I know contributes to something that's really important to me?

Of course, we'd all love to have that extra $50K per year. But when push comes to shove, I've found that most people will do more for that larger purpose than for that extra scratch.

So in my example, I realized that hiring this person would free up my time to devote to doing the work that's really important to me— *eliminating not-enoughness from the world*.

Because when I look at my true mission here on Earth, I realized that "eliminating not-enoughness" is the thing that gets me the most excited and gives me the most purpose—because I believe that the belief in not-enoughness is the #1 cause of most of the suffering we see see in the world today.

So when I was hiring the person whom I eventually hired to delegate this task (and others) to, it was a true Win Cubed—because I Won (I got more free time to do what's important to me), She Won (she got money and the feeling of appreciation), and the World Won (I got to help more people eliminate not-enoughness).

IMPLEMENTING WIN CUBED

You are the leader of your life. You may also be the leader of your team, organization, or company. That's why it's your responsibility to Embrace Your Simplify System both at home and at work.

One way to do this is to consistently communicate Win Cubed with the people in your life. As a leader, it's your responsibility to do this if you want to get better results and help more people with your message.

Unconsciously Successful People have made it a habit to Simplify Their Lives and Streamline Their Businesses on a consistent basis. That's because, just like all of The Power Habits, it's not something you can do just once and be done with it. However, that's also one reason why USPs have so much of what the rest of the world wants.

The great news is, you don't have to be something you're not in order to receive the benefits from Simplifying and Streamlining. You simply have to get started and keep following the steps of this System one day at a time. Yet if you truly want to reach the next level in your life and business—whether to go from zero to six figures, six figures to seven, or seven figures to eight and above—it's crucial to Embrace Your Simplify System, for the simple reason that Information Overload will always be there.

THIS IS ANOTHER REASON USPs HAVE WHAT THE REST OF THE WORLD WANTS.

A "Freedom Lifestyle" is about more than just making more money. While we all want to have more income and more happiness, the Freedom Lifestyle really means helping more people, touching more lives, and making a bigger difference in the world.

That's why installing all five Systems of Support will empower you to enjoy a Freedom Lifestyle without having to sacrifice Who You Really Are. Quite the contrary, when you install your People, Activities, Environment, Introspection, and Simplify Systems, not only will you be able to be and express more of Who You Really Are, but the level of success you attain and the impact on your community (local, national, and yes, perhaps even global) will positively astonish you.

NOAH'S NOTES (IN A NUTSHELL)

1. Because we live in the Information Overload Age, "knowledge" (or information) is no longer power. The true power today lies in Implementation—actually getting things done.

2. That's why Power Habit #7 is **Embrace Your Simplify System**, because it means you'll eliminate what's not truly important to you and start doing things that will help you move to the next level in your life and business.

3. A leader's most important job is to eliminate bottlenecks. The three aspects to consider when confronting bottlenecks are Identification (What's holding me back?), Significance (How important is this to eliminate?), and Cost (What will it cost me if I *don't* eliminate this?)

4. Unconsciously Successful People focus on Win Cubed: I Win, You Win, and the World Wins. This is because most people will do more for meaning (significance) than for money alone.

5. When you Simplify Your Life and Streamline Your Business, you will empower yourself, your team members, your stakeholders, and even your customers to help you reach the next stage of success in your life and business. And you can do it all by being more of Who You Really Are.

#POWERHABITSCHALLENGE #7

1. For your seventh Power Habits Challenge, write a post or share a video about why Embracing Your Simplify System is crucial to your success, and explain one thing you're going to do from this chapter this week, using the hashtag #PowerHabitsChallenge.

2. Be sure to tag me @NoahStJohn so I'll see your post.

CHAPTER 13

POWER HABIT #8: PRACTICE GOAL-FREE ZONES

"We will be more successful in our endeavors if we can let go of the habit of running all the time, and take little pauses to relax and re-center ourselves. We'll also find a lot more joy in living."
— Thich Nhat Hanh

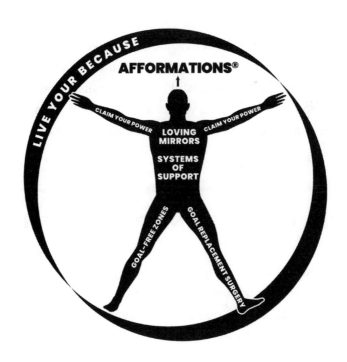

I recently spoke at a business conference where the attendees paid $10,000 just to get in the door. I was amazed by the caliber of the people in attendance. In fact, you probably would have recognized many of them from their frequent television appearances and other highly successful business ventures.

Yet even at this high level of achievement, I was shocked by how many people came up to me after I spoke and told me they felt they were still holding themselves back from their full potential.

For example, one entrepreneur told me that his company brings in more than $20 million a year; but when he started to make it really big, he told me that he started to feel afraid, because nothing like this had ever happened to him.

As a result, he began to sabotage himself. But the most amazing part was that *he could see it happening* and still couldn't stop it. He told me that it was like riding on a train going off the rails, and he felt powerless to stop it.

He told me that he lost about $175,000 in one weekend simply because he didn't know *how to let himself succeed*—which is, of course, exactly what I teach. This highly successful business owner finally said to me, "Noah, it's too bad I didn't hire you as my coach back then, because if I would have done it sooner, it would have saved me a lot of time, money, and heartache!"

WHY GOAL-SETTING SO OFTEN FAILS

As I mentioned in the chapter on Loving Mirrors, the first step of traditional success programs is to *set your goals*. And there's nothing wrong with setting goals—indeed, if you want to reach your goals, you need to first know what they are.

However, as we've seen throughout this book, one of the biggest frustrations people have with traditional success programs is that they so often "set their goals" and then fail to reach them. After helping countless thousands of people just like you reach their goals faster than they ever thought they could, I've identified five major reasons why people fail to meet their goals:

1. You know what your goals are, but don't know how to reach them.

2. You know how to reach your goals, but don't have the resources needed to reach them.

3. You know how to reach your goals and have the resources needed, but are sabotaging your own efforts.

4. You're going after something you don't really want anymore.

5. Your goals are impossible to achieve.

In the first instance, you know what your goals are—for example, you want to attract new customers, hire a new employee, hit your revenue targets, etc. You know what you want, but you're not sure how to get there.

In the second instance, you know what you want and how to get it—for instance, you know your revenue targets and how to do it. The problem in this case is that you don't have the resources—enough time, enough energy, the right relationships, or enough money—to enable you to actually reach your goals.

In the third instance, you have your goals, you know how to reach them, and you have the resources you need—but you're sabotaging your own efforts. This is what's often referred to as "snatching defeat from the jaws of victory."

In the fourth instance, you're actually going after something you don't want anymore. This may have been a goal you used to want, but today you simply don't want it anymore, or you want something else instead.

THESE ARE THE FIVE MAIN REASONS PEOPLE FAIL TO REACH THEIR GOALS.

And in the fifth instance, your goals are simply impossible to achieve. We'll examine these last two instances in the next chapter on Goal Replacement Surgery.

There is, however, something even more subtle going on here. In October 1997, when I discovered the success formula that eventually became The Power Habits® System, I realized that I'd been following the traditional goal-setting advice given by traditional success teachers my whole life. In fact, I had become so indoctrinated to the traditional concepts of goal-setting that I felt guilty whenever I took time off.

I was working harder and harder, yet feeling less and less successful. I also was feeling more and more burned out. In short, I felt like a failure at the age of 30—and I realized that a big reason for that was because whenever I wasn't working, I felt terribly guilty.

That's when I realized the necessity of installing the eighth Power Habit: to **Practice Goal-Free Zones**.

WHY GOAL-FREE ZONES?

A *Goal-Free Zone* is exactly what it sounds like: a time and place where you give yourself *permission to stop setting goals.* If goal-setting is so important to reaching your goals, why is it also important to give yourself permission to STOP setting goals?

The first reason to Practice Goal-Free Zones is *to avoid burnout*. The fact is, if you desire to live a Freedom Lifestyle, you need to give yourself permission to unplug from work. In our natural state, human beings don't expend energy continuously; instead, our energy ebbs and flows like the tide coming in and going out.

In the 1950s, two researchers named William Dement and Nathaniel Kleitman discovered that we sleep in cycles of about 90 minutes at a time, moving from light sleep to deep sleep and back again. They named this pattern *the basic rest–activity cycle.*

A decade later, Professor Kleitman discovered that this cycle also repeats itself during our waking lives. The difference, however, is that during the day, we cycle from a state of *high focus* gradually into a state of *fatigue.*

For example, approximately every 90 minutes during the day, our bodies regularly tell us to take a break by becoming fatigued or needing to stretch. However, in our modern lives, we often ignore these signals and instead push through the fatigue, using stimulants like caffeine, sugar, and our own biological reserves—for example, stress hormones like adrenaline and cortisol.

In another example, Professor K. Anders Ericsson led a study at Florida State University of elite performers, including musicians, actors, athletes, and chess players. In each of these fields, Dr. Ericsson found that the best performers typically practice in uninterrupted, highly focused sessions that last no more than 90 minutes at a time.

They begin in the morning, take a break between sessions, and rarely work for more than four and a half hours in any given day. To maximize gain from long-term practice, Dr. Ericsson concluded in his study, individuals must avoid exhaustion and limit practice to an amount from which they can completely recover on a daily or weekly basis.

PRACTICING GOAL-FREE ZONES WILL HELP YOU AVOID BURNOUT.

Therefore, if you want to maximize your personal productivity, schedule your most demanding work activities in 90-minute intervals throughout your day and develop the habit of unplugging between sessions.

The second reason to Practice Goal-Free Zones is **to reduce the effects of Information Overload.** Unless you decide to live completely off the grid, it's essentially impossible to eliminate the infinite deluge of information coming at us from every direction. You can, however, limit your exposure to it by Practicing Goal-Free Zones.

GOAL-FREE ZONES CAN HELP YOU REDUCE INFORMATION OVERLOAD.

Studies have shown that the human brain was simply not designed to handle the non-stop stimulus that so many people subject themselves to on a daily basis. For example, a recent survey by the Alliance of Automobile Manufacturers found that 70 percent of Americans sleep with their cell phone within arm's reach, 61 percent check their phones every hour, and a whopping 90 percent of drivers keep their mobile phone in their hand, lap, cupholder, or on the passenger seat while driving their cars.

When you combine Information Overload with the fact that most people never actually unplug from it, you've got a recipe for why so many people feel overwhelmed, overworked, and stressed out all the time. Hence, Practicing Goal-Free Zones will empower you to lessen these negative emotions.

The third, and perhaps most important reason of all to Practice Goal-Free Zones, is **to reconnect with your Authentic Self.** Have you ever noticed that your best ideas tend NOT to come when you're staring at your smartphone or laptop? I'd wager that your best, most creative and inspiring ideas come to you when you're walking, relaxing, journaling, meditating, or even (ahem) in the shower. (After all, The Shower That Changed Everything is one of the main reasons I've helped people like you make so much money and fulfill your true mission on Earth!)

When you're staring at a screen or constantly working, it's hard to hear the "still, small voice" of your intuition or Authentic Self. In addition, you need to realize that *your worth does not come from your achievements.* Many people, especially high-performing individuals, subconsciously believe that they're only worthwhile when they're achieving things or winning awards or have lots of money.

You need to truly realize that your worth does not come from your achievements. It's one thing to say that and another to actually believe it. As I often tell my coaching clients, if you keep your nose to the grindstone too long, eventually you'll have no nose.

HOW TO USE THE N.M.U.I. PRINCIPLE

I created this book using a process that I teach my $100,000 VIP Coaching Clients, and I'd like to share it with you, too. There is a method that I've developed over the last 20-plus years of helping people like you to add six and seven figures to their businesses, and it's called **The N.M.U.I. Principle.**

Let me give you an example. When Nightingale-Conant asked me to write this book, I wanted to make it something very special, something different from my previous books. However, I also wanted to give you, the reader, the benefit of my 20-plus years of real-world experience helping people just like you achieve their dream of living a Freedom Lifestyle.

GOAL-FREE ZONES WILL HELP YOU RECONNECT WITH YOUR AUTHENTIC SELF.

Therefore, I decided to create this book using *The N.M.U.I. Principle*—which stands for **Ninety-Minute Uninterrupted Intervals.**

THE N.M.U.I. PRINCIPLE CAN EXPLODE YOUR DAILY PRODUCTIVITY.

What I did was, every morning during my writing of this book, I would sit down at my computer and start writing. I would work in NMUIs, or Ninety-Minute Uninterrupted Intervals. During these NMUIs, I turned off my phone, didn't check my email, never looked at social media, and focused completely on writing this book for 90 minutes at a time. That way, I consciously eliminated all distractions and was able to work very efficiently.

Then, after about 90 minutes of uninterrupted work, I would physically get up from my computer, take a brisk walk, or sometimes take a 15- to 20-minute power nap. Then I'd come back to writing again, feeling refreshed and rejuvenated.

Sometimes I'd go for a walk outside and enjoy the sunshine, and suddenly an idea would pop into my head. What's fascinating is how many of my creative ideas that appear in this book would occur to me, not as I was working at my computer screen, but during my Goal-Free Zones.

Other times, I would wake up at four or five o'clock in the morning with a creative idea that I just had to share with you. So, I'd get up, write it down, and then go back to bed.

(By the way, be sure that you have the means to record your ideas when inspiration strikes—because creative ideas can be fleeting, and you don't want to lose them. Therefore, be sure to capture your ideas on paper, or record it on your phone or other recording device, the moment you have them, or risk losing them forever.)

Even though my Power Habits® System represents more than 25 years of real-world research and firsthand experience with countless thousands of coaching clients and mastermind students—people just like you from around the world—the result is that, because I've installed these Power Habits in my own life, I completed writing this book *in less than 90 days.* And guess what? It wasn't even stressful.

One other fun note: My editor told me that since reading this book, she has also adopted this habit of Practicing Goal-Free Zones and working in NMUIs, and she told me that her productivity has skyrocketed too!

Bottom line: When you develop this habit of Practicing Goal-Free Zones, coupled with The N.M.U.I. Principle, you'll be amazed at what you can accomplish.

HOW TO PRACTICE GOAL-FREE ZONES

Here's an exercise I like to do at my private workshops called "Practicing Goal-Free Zones." First, answer these questions:

1. What are my favorite Goal-Free Zone activities?

2. When and where can I do them?

3. What negative beliefs do I have about doing Goal-Free Zones?

4. What will happen if I don't Practice Goal-Free Zones?

Beginning with Question #1, what do you like to do when you unplug from work? Maybe you enjoy meditating, journaling, walking, bicycling, jogging, exercising, golfing, or taking a nap? Be sure to list Goal-Free Zone activities that you actually like.

By the way, I suggest NOT listing "watching TV" as a Goal-Free Zone activity, because I want you to be literally "unplugged." When you watch TV, although it may be mindless, it's really not rejuvenating. You usually don't feel refreshed

BE SURE YOU DO GOAL-FREE ZONES THAT YOU ACTUALLY LIKE.

after watching TV. That's because so much of the programming on TV tends to sap, rather than renew, our energy, as it's not really engaging our minds and certainly isn't giving us the time to get in touch with our Authentic Selves.

IF YOU WANT DIFFERENT RESULTS, YOU MUST FIRST CHANGE YOUR HABITS.

Then, answer the question of when and where you can Practice Your Goal-Free Zones. Of course, you'll want to make sure that you create the ability to Practice Goal-Free Zones when it's actually convenient to do them: in your workspace during the day, or in your home office if that's where you work.

Of course, some will say that it's not convenient or that your boss won't let you Practice Goal-Free Zones. That's one reason many companies and organizations hire me to do private workshops. Because, while it can be difficult to change people's minds about the benefits of Goal-Free Zones from the inside, once leaders and managers start to see the benefits for themselves—increased productivity, fewer illness-related absences, higher retention, etc.—they're usually quick to adopt these Power Habits and empower their employees to do the same. (To book a private workshop with me to help your team, company, or organization install my Power Habits® System, go to **www.NoahStJohn.com/private-workshop**)

Then, determine what negative beliefs you have about Practicing Goal-Free Zones. For example, maybe you think: "I don't have the time. I can't afford to stop. My parents taught me to work hard. My boss will never let me do this. I don't have any time because of the kids." Whatever your reasons/excuses are, write them down.

Then, identify what will happen if you *don't* Practice Goal-Free Zones. Remember that *pain* is often the best motivator. By now, you know that if you keep doing what you're doing, you're going to keep getting what you're getting.

IF YOU WANT DIFFERENT RESULTS, DO THIS FIRST

My experience of working with individual clients and organizations around the world for the last 20-plus years has exposed the following truth: *If you want different results, you must first change your habits.* There's really no way around that simple fact.

For example, if you hired me do a private workshop or to be your coach and told me, "I want better results"—and you were currently unhappy and not getting the results you wanted, and I told you to keep doing the same thing, that wouldn't do you much good, now would it?

It would be like the overweight person who hired a personal trainer and then the trainer said to them, "Oh, you don't need to work out. Just keep eating what you're eating and doing what you're doing. I'm sure it will all work out."

The irony of my work, of course, is that while we human beings all want things to be different, WE don't want to change in order to make those changes happen. In other words: *we want THINGS to change; but WE don't want to change.*

In The Power Habits® System, I've shown you exactly why this happens—because of the nature of the brain itself to stick with habits that it has already installed. That's why it's so common for people to believe that we don't have to change in order to get the things we desire.

WE HUMANS WANT THINGS TO CHANGE, BUT WE DON'T WANT TO CHANGE.

However, you know the truth: if you want different results—whether it's to lose weight, make more money, grow your business, or be happy—you know that you have to do different things. It just sucks that that's the way it is. That's why it's my job as your Power Habits® Mentor to help you get there faster, easier, and with a lot less stress.

I hate to be this obvious, but if you want to be highly successful, then you need to start doing what highly successful people do. The problem, as we've seen, is that the majority of highly successful people are also the Unconsciously Successful People (USPs) whom I talked about in an earlier chapter. That means that while they may tell you some of the things they did to become successful, they'll always leave something out. The irony is that *they always leave the good stuff out.*

Think about it this way: if someone is 100 times more successful than you are, are they 100 times smarter than you? Do they have 100 times the education you have? Do they work 100 times harder or 100 times more hours than you do? Of course not, because none of these things are even possible.

The essential difference between highly successful people and everyone else is that they have (unconsciously) adapted The Power Habits® of Unconsciously Successful People. That's why I give keynote speeches, lead private workshops, and host live seminars—so that finally, the rest of us can have the same advantages as the USPs that they'll never be able to give us.

THE GOAL-FREE ZONE HABIT LOOP

Now let's see how to use the Habit Loop to help you Practice Goal-Free Zones.

First, identify your Cue for when you could Practice Goal-Free Zones in your day. For example, you could say, "Well, every day I feel tired at around three o'clock in the afternoon." That's a Cue right there.

Now when this Cue occurs for you, I'll bet you also have a Routine—for example, maybe you just power through it, drink another cup of coffee, reach for a snack, check your phone, or surf the Internet.

But are any of these Routines the best solution to maximize your productivity? Probably not. So, let's install a new, more empowering Routine.

How about, when you have the Cue of feeling tired in the afternoon, developing a new Routine like...

✓ Standing up and stretching

✓ Taking a brisk walk

✓ Taking a 15-minute power nap

✓ Talking with a friend

✓ Eating a healthy snack instead of junk food (and yes, you know the difference)

✓ Drinking water instead of coffee

Any of these healthy alternatives can become your new Routine.

Then, what's the Reward for doing your new Routine?

You're probably going to feel refreshed, rejuvenated, renewed, stimulated, more creative; you're also going to lower your stress and increase your productivity, and I'll bet you'll get a lot more done in a lot less time. Nice Rewards, aren't they?

Then, write your new Beliefs in form of Afformations®.

For example, you could Afform:

✓ *Why do I love Practicing Goal-Free Zones?*

INSTALLING HEALTHY ROUTINES WILL HELP YOU PRACTICE GOAL-FREE ZONES.

✓ *Why is it so easy for me to Practice Goal-Free Zones?*

✓ *Why do I love my new healthy habits?*

✓ *Why do I love being so productive and focused at work?*

By the way, many forward-thinking companies have finally caught on to the fact that human beings are not robots and can't work non-stop for eight hours a day. For example, leading companies like Google, Zappos, Nike, British Airways, Viacom, and even Pizza Hut are now providing nap rooms for their employees and actually encouraging napping on the job, because they realize that providing napping facilities for their employees is a Win Cubed (see what I did there?) that makes for a happier, healthier, and more productive workforce.

And would you like to hear a list of some of history's most famous nappers? They include:

✓ Thomas Edison

✓ Winston Churchill

✓ John D. Rockefeller

✓ Albert Einstein

✓ Leonardo da Vinci

Presidents John F. Kennedy, Dwight Eisenhower, Ronald Reagan, and Lyndon B. Johnson all took naps while in office, as did First Lady Eleanor Roosevelt. So, if you enjoy napping as your Goal-Free Zones (like me), you're in great company!

Bottom line: When you begin to Practice Goal-Free Zones, you'll increase your productivity, improve your creativity, and reduce much of the daily stress you're facing today. So start to Practice Goal-Free Zones and watch your productivity—and your peace of mind—skyrocket!

NOAH'S NOTES (IN A NUTSHELL)

1. Traditional success teachers told us to "set your goals" if you want to achieve more. While that's not exactly wrong, the problem is that millions of people have set goals that they failed to accomplish.

2. There are five main reasons we fail to accomplish our goals. However, one of the subtle reasons many people fail to reach their goals is that they feel guilty when they're not working to reach their goals.

3. That's why Power Habit #8 is **Practice Goal-Free Zones**— because it means giving yourself permission to stop setting goals throughout your day.

4. Benefits of Practicing Goal-Free Zones include: avoiding burnout, reducing the effects of Information Overload, and reconnecting with your Authentic Self.

5. I created this book (as well as my online programs and other products) using **The N.M.U.I. Principle**—working in *Ninety-Minute Uninterrupted Intervals* and then taking a Goal-Free Zone between work times.

6. If you want different results, you have to change your habits.

7. The truth is that we humans want THINGS to be different, but WE don't want to change. The only problem is, that has never worked and will never work on planet Earth. That's why I created The Power Habits® System—so that everyone who wants better results can start to implement The Power Habits® of Unconsciously Successful People.

8. To book a private workshop with me to help your team, company, or organization install these Power Habits for

better results with less time, money, and effort, go to **www. NoahStJohn.com/private-workshop**

#POWERHABITSCHALLENGE #8

1. For your eighth Power Habits Challenge, write a post or share a video about why Practicing Goal-Free Zones is crucial to your success, and describe one thing you're going to do from this chapter this week, using the hashtag #PowerHabitsChallenge.

2. Be sure to tag me @NoahStJohn so I'll see your post.

CHAPTER 14

POWER HABIT #9: PERFORM GOAL REPLACEMENT SURGERY

"A nail is driven out by another nail;
habit is overcome by habit."
— Desiderius Erasmus

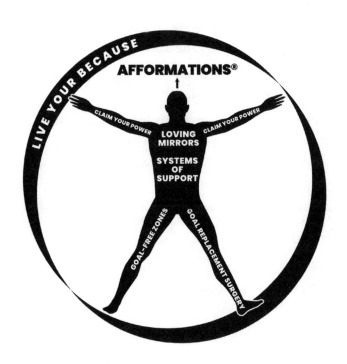

Stacey was a successful chiropractor in Canada who loved her job. She enjoyed working with patients and seeing them get healthier. However, she had a problem: as hard as she worked, Stacey could never seem to have the financial freedom she saw other entrepreneurs enjoying.

She was working long hours and making good money; however, she realized that if she kept doing what she was doing, she was going to keep getting the same results—working harder for the same amount of money year after year.

Then a friend recommended to Stacey that she attend one of my live seminars, where I teach people how to live the "Freedom Lifestyle" of their dreams. She came to my event somewhat skeptical that I could help her achieve her goals. But she was open and coachable and willing to try something new in order to get the results she was looking for.

At the end of my seminars, there's often a line of people waiting to talk to me. Stacey and her husband were in the line and I could tell something was on her mind. She said to me, "This all sounds great, Noah—but I'm not sure how it applies to me."

"What do you mean?" I asked.

"Well," she said, "I want to grow my business and make more money, but I'm not sure how to use your system to do it."

"Let me ask you a question," I said. "You love helping people, right?"

"Of course," she said.

"And when patients come to see you, you give them information that helps them, right?"

"Yes," she said.

"And right now, you share that information with each patient individually?"

"Right."

"Well, do you see the problem?" I asked.

"No," she said.

"Let me explain," I said...

Are you feeling kind of like Stacey was? Like this all sounds great, but you're not exactly sure how to apply this to your life?

Well, let me ask YOU the same thing I asked Stacey...

Do you enjoy helping people?

Do you want to do something with your life, but you're not quite sure what it is or how to get there?

Are you looking for a simple way to help more people, make more money, and have more freedom?

If you answered "yes" to any of these questions, then you need to install the ninth Power Habit, **Perform Goal Replacement Surgery**.

WHAT IS GOAL REPLACEMENT SURGERY?

When I wrote my first book *Permission to Succeed®* in 1997 and subsequently developed The Power Habits® System over the last two decades, I realized that in addition to the reasons I mentioned in the previous chapter, there are three other, hidden reasons why so many people fail to reach their goals:

1. They're going after goals they don't really want anymore; or

2. They're going after impossible goals; or

3. They're going after someone else's goals.

I call these three types of goals *Non-Attainable Goals*, because they are either: a) not attainable—i.e., not able to be realized—or b) unbelievably unsatisfying.

That's when I realized that the Power Habit of Performing Goal Replacement Surgery was so crucial to success for individuals, teams, organizations, and corporations large and small.

Goal Replacement Surgery is the strategic process of doing three things:

1. Clarifying the goals you're currently going after;

2. Identifying whether your goals are Attainable or Non-Attainable Goals.

3. Eliminating the latter and focusing your time, money, and effort on the former.

Let's examine each of the Non-Attainable Goal types and discover why it's crucial to stop going after them by Performing Goal Replacement Surgery.

REPLACE YOUR OUTDATED GOALS

The first type of Non-Attainable Goal is the goal that you don't really want anymore—what I call **Outdated Goals**.

For example, before I became a keynote speaker and bestselling author, I was employed as a professional ballet dancer. (Yes, I'm pretty sure I'm the only person in this business development and personal growth industry who once made a living lifting ballerinas.) So my #1 goal during this time was to become the next Mikhail Baryshnikov.

I worked harder than anyone in the company to achieve that goal. I came in early and stayed late. I practiced for hours and hours on end. My body was in constant pain, both physical and emotional, for so long that I didn't even know there was another way to live.

Unfortunately, I never achieved that goal of becoming the next Baryshnikov—for one, because no dancer before or since had as much raw talent as he did, but also because I suffered a career-ending injury at the age of 21 that forced me to retire from professional dancing long before I was ready to.

THIS IS A GREAT EXAMPLE OF AN OUTDATED GOAL.

So during my teens and early 20s, I had this goal that I really, really worked hard at yet ended up not achieving. So what if today, in my 50s, I decided that I wanted to resurrect that goal and become the next Baryshnikov?

The answer is that there's no way I would achieve it—because, as I've stated several times before, in the game of life, Father Time is undefeated. So this would be a simple example of an Outdated Goal.

REPLACE YOUR IMPOSSIBLE GOALS

It's also an example of an **Impossible Goal**. An Impossible Goal is just what it sounds like—a goal that can't be accomplished.

Now, I know you're not used to hearing something like that in a business and personal growth book. You're used to hearing things like "If you can conceive it, you can achieve it" and "There's nothing you can't do when you set your mind to it."

And those may be true for the majority of our goals. However, the truth is that there are some things you simply can't do. Not only that, but to continue to go after them would constitute a waste of your time, money, and effort.

For example, for years I had a goal of "making everyone happy." In other words, I truly believed that if I worked hard enough, I could "make

ARE YOU GOING AFTER ANY OF THESE IMPOSSIBLE GOALS?

everyone happy" and then they (everyone) would like me. How do you think THAT turned out?

As you can imagine, three things ended up happening:

1. I tried to make everyone happy by ignoring my own feelings and never standing up for myself or what I wanted or believed in.

2. I discovered that no matter how hard I tried, I couldn't make everyone happy.

3. I later found out that no matter what I did or didn't do, I couldn't actually make ANYONE happy.

The technical truth is that you can't "make" another person happy. Why? Because each human being is responsible for their own happiness or unhappiness. That means that no one can "make" you happy, just as no one can "make" you unhappy. As Abraham Lincoln said: "Most folks are about as happy as they make up their minds to be."

The point is that the goal of "making everyone happy"—indeed, to "make" ANYONE happy—is, by its very nature, impossible. For example, have you ever been in a relationship with a person who, no matter what you do for them, no matter how much you give them, they're never happy—because it's "not enough"? (I can hear some of you saying, "Noah, have you been following me around?")

Of course, you and I can *influence* another person's happiness. For example, we can appreciate, show kindness, express gratitude, and many of the other things I talked about in the chapter on Upgrading Your People System.

Yet there's an enormous difference between *influence* and *control*. To think that we can control someone else's emotions is ridiculous, even laughable. However, millions of people wake up every morning and unwittingly do what I used to do—try to make everyone else happy, because they think it's their job to do so.

Please note that most Impossible Goals are also *unconscious* goals—meaning, the person doesn't consciously realize they're going after them. For instance, see if you can recognize going after any of these Impossible (unconscious) Goals:

✓ *I have to make everyone happy.*

✓ *I have to make (my spouse, my kids, my boss) happy.*

✓ *I have to be perfect.*

✓ *I shouldn't make mistakes.*

✓ *I have to close 100 percent of my prospects.*

Why is it so important to stop going after Impossible Goals such as these? Because if you're going after Impossible Goals—even if you're not doing it consciously—it means that you have less psychic energy to use in pursuit of your Attainable Goals.

Look at the example of "I have to close 100 percent of my prospects." I used to think that too when I first got into business. When I launched SuccessClinic.com in my college dorm room in 1997, I had zero experience in sales, marketing, or running my own business. Naturally, I thought that successful business owners closed 100 percent of their sales opportunities.

So when I'd make a great presentation and someone wouldn't buy, I would get very depressed and beat myself up, because I thought that I had "failed." It wasn't until going through this process myself that I realized that NO ONE, not even the greatest salesperson on Earth, closes 100 percent of their prospects. So it was a waste of time and energy to beat myself up for not reaching that Impossible Goal, since it was, in fact, Impossible.

Now, you might be saying, "But Noah, I don't have any of these Impossible Goals." Great! Just realize that none of these Impossible Goals occur consciously.

For example, no one wakes up in the morning and says, "Wow, it's a beautiful day. I think I'll try to make everyone happy, sell 100 percent of my prospects, and never make a mistake today. Oh, and if I don't do all that, I'm a failure."

The reason we beat ourselves up for not reaching these Impossible Goals is because they lie below the surface of our conscious awareness—which means we unknowingly react when things go wrong or when we fall short of our goals.

REPLACE SOMEONE ELSE'S GOALS

The next set of Non-Attainable Goals is **Someone Else's Goals**. For example, did you hear the story about the guy who became a dentist because his father was a dentist because his father was a dentist...so he was expected to be a dentist? Yet what this guy really wanted to be was a clothing designer.

So let me ask you: how successful do you think this guy's dental practice was? Furthermore, how *happy* do you think he was in his work? Exactly: not very and not very.

The point is that many of us have had expectations heaped upon us by others. As well-meaning as they might be, if you're going after a goal that someone else placed upon you, you're either going to be not very successful, not very happy, or both.

Surprisingly, this is a very common theme in, of all things, Disney movies—specifically, for Disney princesses. For example, think of the expectations placed on the following Disney characters:

✓ *Cinderella* was expected to stay home and clean.

- ✓ Ariel (*The Little Mermaid*) was expected to be a good little mermaid.

- ✓ Belle (*Beauty and the Beast*) was expected to be a good "little wife."

- ✓ Jasmine (*Aladdin*) was expected to marry a prince.

- ✓ *Mulan* was expected to follow her family's traditions and not, you know, go to war.

I would argue that most Disney movies follow this same framework: hero (or heroine) has expectations placed upon them by their elders/tribe/family; hero/heroine rebels against those expectations; hero/heroine faces overwhelming odds and triumphs in the end.

Okay, that's the movies—but what about real life? Remember Stacey, the client to whom I introduced you at the beginning of this chapter? Let's go back to that scene at my live seminar (cue the harp music)…

"You love helping people, right?" I asked her.

"Of course," she said.

"And when patients come to see you, you give them information that helps them, right?"

"Yes," she said.

"And right now, you share that information with each patient individually?"

"Right."

"Well, do you see the problem?" I asked.

"No," she said.

"Let me explain," I said. "The problem is that there's only one of you, and right now, you can only help one person at a time. But what if I taught you how to package all that knowledge you have in your head and sell it to the world—so you could help not just the people in your community, but around the world?"

She stood there with her mouth agape.

"I never thought of that before," she said.

Stacey told me that she was a fourth-generation chiropractor and that no one in her family had ever done anything like that.

"That's what I'm here for," I said.

The point of the story is that because Stacey didn't know anything other than the "one to one" model, her income was, by definition, limited. Stacey decided to hire me as her coach on the spot, and decided to become one of my VIP Coaching Clients. After I coached her and taught her how to add "one-to-many" packages to her business, **her business DOUBLED in less than 18 months.**

This is just one of the many benefits you can get from attending our live events and hiring me as your business and personal growth coach— because all too often, we're too close to our own problems to be able to see the way out.

YOUR HABITS REVEAL YOUR PRINCIPLES

In *The 7 Habits of Highly Effective People*, Stephen Covey writes about the nature of principles. He talks about principles like *fairness, integrity, honesty, human dignity, service, excellence, potential, and growth.* "Principles," he argues, "are not processes; they are fundamental guidelines for human conduct."

Covey writes, "Principles are essentially inarguable because they are self-evident. One way to quickly grasp the self-evident nature of principles is to simply consider the absurdity of attempting to live an effective life based on their opposites. I don't think anybody would seriously consider unfairness, deceit, uselessness, mediocrity, or degeneration to be a solid foundation for lasting happiness."

YOUR DAILY HABITS REVEAL YOUR PRINCIPLES.

In short, your habits reveal the principles you choose to live by. Ask yourself: "What principles do I choose to live by, and how will I express those principles today?"

When you follow The Power Habits® System, you will begin to reveal more of your Authentic Self—that part of you that deeply understands the nature of principles like honesty, fairness, integrity, and love.

This simple habit of *expressing your principles through your daily habits* will greatly determine how quickly you reach your goals and how many people will support you along the way.

That's why Performing Goal Replacement Surgery is one of the most important Power Habits you can do. Why? Because if your time, money, and energy are being used trying to achieve Outdated Goals, Impossible Goals, or Someone Else's Goals, you won't have the psychic, physical, or financial resources to achieve the goals you really DO want.

NOAH'S NOTES (IN A NUTSHELL)

1. Many people are going after goals they don't want anymore, or goals they thought they should do, or goals that someone else told them to do. I call these types of goals *Non-Attainable Goals*, because even if you do achieve them, you won't be happy.

2. That's why Power Habit #9 is **Perform Goal Replacement Surgery**—because it means stopping yourself from going after Non-Attainable Goals.

3. The three types of Non-Attainable Goals are: *Outdated Goals* (goals that have passed their expiration date), *Impossible Goals* (goals that can't be achieved by a human being), and *Someone Else's Goals* (the expectations of others).

4. Performing Goal Replacement Surgery means asking yourself if any of the goals to which you're currently giving psychic or physical energy are Outdated, Impossible, or Someone Else's, and systematically replacing them with Attainable Goals that you actually want.

5. If you'd like to attend our Freedom Lifestyle Experience Live event, so you can discover the secrets to master your Inner Game and Outer Game of Success, claim your **"Buy 1, Bring a Friend FREE"** tickets now at **www.FreedomLifeX.com**

#POWERHABITSCHALLENGE #9

1. For your ninth Power Habits Challenge, write a post or share a video about why Performing Goal Replacement Surgery is crucial to your success, and identify one thing you're going to do this week to start doing it, using the hashtag #PowerHabitsChallenge.

2. Be sure to tag me @NoahStJohn so I'll see your post.

CHAPTER 15

POWER HABIT #10:
CLAIM YOUR POWER

*"The habit of being happy enables one to be freed
from the domination of outward conditions."*
— Robert Louis Stevenson

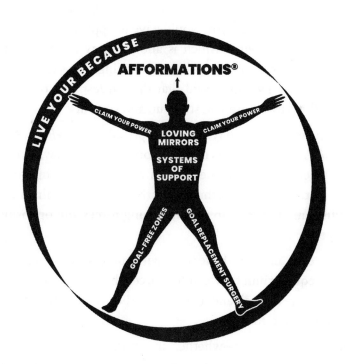

In the 1940s, a German-American psychologist named Kurt Lewin came up with a theory of human behavior he called the Force-Field Analysis Model. It sounds really fancy, but it's actually simple to understand. Imagine that you're sitting in your favorite chair in your home or office right now. What exactly is keeping you in that chair?

The first thing keeping you in your chair is the force of *gravity*, which is pushing you down toward the center of the Earth. Let's call this force a *driving force*. The second force is the chair itself, which provides an *opposing force*—that is, a force that's pushing you up against the force of gravity and stopping you from falling to the ground.

While you're sitting in your chair, you're in a state of *equilibrium*—which is the state of balance or status quo; which means that right now, you're not falling to the ground, but you're also not floating up into the sky.

Now imagine that you want to move out of this state of equilibrium. What could you do? Well, you would have to apply a force that's greater than the force of gravity—which is another way of saying, stand up. However, it does require an additional driving force for you to stand up—which is why I've often said that the hardest part of any exercise program is the part where you stand up and start it.

Congratulations, you have just completed a *Force-Field Analysis.* A Force-Field Analysis consists of three core concepts: driving forces (the power or energy behind something in motion), opposing forces (also known as restraining forces, the energy that stops something in motion), and equilibrium, the state in which driving forces and opposing forces are balanced.

So, what does all of this have to do with success? Right now, you exist in a state of equilibrium between the forces that want you to experience change (driving forces) and the forces that don't want anything to change (restraining forces).

If change is to occur—whether in an individual, team, company, organization, or any human relationship—the point of equilibrium must be moved; yet this can only be done by *adding conditions favorable to the change* or by *reducing the forces that are resisting the change.*

When driving forces become stronger than restraining forces, the point of equilibrium changes—for instance, you use the energy in your body to stand up from your chair. However, as long as restraining forces remain stronger than driving forces, the point of equilibrium does not change. That's what makes the phrase "couch potato" so accurate—a potato doesn't have enough energy to, um, move.

YOUR SUCCESS IS DETERMINED BY DRIVING FORCES AND RESTRAINING FORCES.

There will always be driving forces that make change appear attractive (*Hey, I'd better get up before I turn into a couch potato!*) just as there will always be restraining forces that work to keep things just the way they are there (*Nah, I'm good right here.*).

Successful change, then, can only be achieved by strengthening driving forces, weakening restraining forces, or both. That's why the tenth Power Habit is called **Claim Your Power**.

WHAT DOES IT MEAN TO CLAIM YOUR POWER?

Over the last 20-plus years of helping people just like you to add six, seven, and eight figures to their business, I have learned that there are three ways change can occur in a human being, as well as in any human relationship like a team, business, or organization:

1. Increase the power of the driving forces; or

2. Decrease the power of the restraining forces; or

3. A combination of the two.

That's why, when I coach individuals, teams, or organizations to reach their goals faster, easier, and with less effort, one of the places I start is with a variation of Lewin's Force-Field Analysis—because then the client and I can quickly analyze the driving and restraining forces at work that are creating the current state of equilibrium.

Keep in mind that when we're talking about human behavior, we're not talking about logical, rational creatures. We're talking about people who are driven by emotion and habit—in fact, who are driven by the very Habit Loop I've been showing you in this book.

Therefore, here is a simplified version of the Force-Field Analysis Tool I use with my coaching clients, so you can start to identify the driving and restraining forces at work in your life or business right now:

Step 1: Identify your current state of equilibrium (your Current Perceived Reality). Where are you right now in relation to where you want to be?

Step 2: Specify where you want to be (your New Desired Reality). What's your "pot of gold" at the end of the rainbow?

Step 3: List the driving forces acting to support the change you want. These could include things like your own personal drive, motivation, and other resources. These forces are "your foot on the gas."

Step 4: List the restraining forces acting to block the change. These could include things like fear, uncertainty, or simply not knowing what to do or whom to talk to. These forces are "your foot on the brake."

WHEN I COACH INDIVIDUALS, TEAMS, OR ORGANIZATIONS, WE OFTEN START WITH A FORCE-FIELD ANALYSIS.

Step 5: Brainstorm ways to increase the driving forces and decrease the restraining forces. Identify all the resources you will need to reach your New Desired Reality. These can include hiring a coach, working with a mentor, enrolling in courses, and so on.

Step 6: Choose one force to work on and get to work. For example, if you decide to hire a coach, decide whom you're going to hire and get started. Then go to the next step, and so on, until you've exhausted all possibilities. (See also the Recommended Resources in the back of this book.)

Go ahead and do this exercise right now for the New Desired Reality you'd like to experience in your life, business, career, or relationships. (I'll wait.)

After doing this exercise, you should have a solid plan of action of what to do next to reach your New Desired Reality. However, keep in mind that if you do nothing to change the balance of your driving and restraining forces, then the state of equilibrium won't change—which means that reaching your goal will remain very difficult.

Therefore, your first order of business should be to reduce the restraining forces, increase the driving forces, or both. In my experience, while there are numerous driving and restraining forces that can act upon an individual, team, or organization, there are two major ones I'll address in this book—first, the driving force of "I'll show you" and the restraining force of fear.

HOW "I'LL SHOW YOU" CREATED THE G.O.A.T.

I grew up in Kennebunkport, Maine, in the 1970s, and since there was no Internet back then, there wasn't much to do except

IF YOU WANT CHANGE TO OCCUR, YOU MUST DO ONE OF THESE THREE THINGS.

watch sports. So I grew up watching two teams: the Boston Red Sox and the New England Patriots.

USE THE POWER OF "I'LL SHOW YOU" TO DRIVE YOU TO SUCCESS.

There was just one problem: both teams sucked. So seeing the New England Patriots become the most successful team in all of professional sports in this century has been more than a little satisfying.

Tom Brady, the quarterback of my hometown New England Patriots, grew up idolizing Joe Montana of the San Francisco 49ers.

Yet today, with a record-setting six Super Bowl rings (at the time of this writing), Tom Brady has far out-Joe-Montana'd Joe Montana to become the undisputed G.O.A.T.—"Greatest Of All Time."

However, Tom Brady was drafted in the sixth round of the 2000 NFL draft—the 199th player selected. To put that in perspective, it means that the highly paid coaches and scouts of the National Football League, in their infinite wisdom, determined that there were 198 players BETTER than Tom Brady that year.

When he talks about that day, Tom still gets teary-eyed. And (as of this writing) he still plays with a chip on his shoulder, as if to say, "I'll show YOU how great I am!"

Therefore, when people dismiss you or discourage you, you have two choices: believe them and give up, or play YOUR game and prove that they're wrong.

That's the power of "I'll show you."

Unconsciously Successful People use the phrase "I'll show you" to drive themselves to succeed when everyone else says it can't be done. That's why a big part of Claiming Your Power means understanding how you respond when people tell you that you can't do something.

For instance, when someone says to you, "What makes you think you can do that?" you can either get discouraged, or you can use it to motivate you. The trick is to use the power of "I'll show you" to your advantage. Use it to create a driving force that will overcome any restraining force that's holding you back. Never underestimate the power of "I'll show you."

THE RESTRAINING FORCE OF FEAR

Do you know what *fear* really is? Well, here's what fear is NOT: fear is NOT "false evidence appearing real."

I know you've heard that acronym a million times before and were probably expecting me to say it, right? Well, the truth is, some clever speaker came up with that acronym many years ago—and unfortunately, it's become one of the most widely accepted clichés in the personal growth industry.

FEAR IS THE EMOTIONAL EFFECT OF THE PERCEIVED ABSENCE OF CONTROL.

The problem is, that's not what fear is at all. Here's what fear really is: fear is a human emotion that occurs when you anticipate or expect that something or someone may hurt you. In other words, fear is *the anticipation or expectation of pain.*

When you fear something, you're essentially saying to yourself, "Hey, what if doing this causes me pain?" Ironically, the purpose of the emotion of fear is to protect you from getting hurt. Of course, one of the big problems with fear is that while it's a real human emotion that's there to protect you, it can also hold you back from becoming the person you were meant to be.

UNCONSCIOUSLY SUCCESSFUL PEOPLE TAKE ACTION, EVEN IN THE FACE OF FEAR.

We experience the emotion of fear when we perceive that we're not in control. In other words, fear is the emotional effect of the perceived absence of personal control. Therefore, there's an inverse relationship between control and fear—the more control we have over our lives, the less fear we feel; the less control we think we have, the more fear we feel.

One of the most basic human fears is *the fear of rejection*—the fear that "If I do this, that person will reject or not like me." Why is this one of the most basic human fears? Centuries ago, we humans lived in tribes as a means of survival. Imagine you were living in tribal days and you did something bad—something that was considered a crime against the tribe. In tribal cultures, the worst punishment was not death, but *banishment from the tribe.*

That's because if you were banished from the tribe, there was very little chance that you were going to survive on your own out there in the wild. So, how does that relate to the fear of rejection in our modern world? It shows up all the time in social settings: our business life, our career, at home, and in our family life.

For example, imagine that you're a salesperson and you want to increase your sales (what salesperson doesn't?). What can you do to increase your sales? Well, one way is to call your current customers and see if they want to buy something else from you.

What does the average salesperson do when they have this thought? Their next thought might be something like, "Well, I don't want to bother them. They probably wouldn't be interested anyway. If they wanted something, they would have called me already." In other words, the average salesperson knows what to do but *doesn't do it*—because they've given in to their fear of rejection.

Contrast this with what highly successful salespeople do. Highly successful salespeople might hear that same head trash that says, "I don't want to bother them"; they might feel that same fear of rejection in the pit of their stomach. But highly successful salespeople *call their customers anyway.*

That's why one of the main differences between Unconsciously Successful People and everyone else is that USPs feel the fear but take action anyway—even in the face of fear.

HOW TO TAKE ACTION IN THE FACE OF FEAR

Since we now know that fear is nothing more than the anticipation of pain, one of the easiest ways to take action in the face of fear is to *emotionally accept the pain* that might occur as a result of taking the action.

For example, in my younger days, I didn't have a "fear" of rejection; I had a *certainty* of rejection. When you grow up as a scrawny, geeky kid with Coke bottle glasses, acne, and shoulder-width hair, it's not hard to see why. I was painfully shy and afraid to talk to just about anyone—because I was sure they wouldn't like me.

Many years later, I began to understand that almost everyone has pretty much the same fear of rejection that I had. This helped me see that I really wasn't different from anyone else. Then, when I was in social settings and would feel that same fear—er, certainty—of rejection, I started doing a mental exercise where I would imagine the person I was talking to rejecting me and then imagined how I would feel afterward.

Once I emotionally accepted the pain of getting rejected by a total stranger—someone who didn't even know me anyway—I actually felt *more in control* of the situation, because I realized it didn't hurt as badly as

I thought it would. Developing this mental habit gave me the confidence to be myself with the people I met.

> I WAS ABSOLUTELY POSITIVE SHE WOULD REJECT ME.

One day when I was 40 years old, doing this exercise even gave me the confidence to call a gorgeous blonde I had met and ask her to go on a date with me. I knew she was totally out of my league and was certain to reject me, because she was so pretty and smart and likeable. I was absolutely positive she would say no, and I had emotionally accepted that fact before I even made the call.

To my utter astonishment, she said yes. A short time after that, I asked her to marry me—and to my great delight, she said yes again. That's the story of how I met and married my beautiful wife, Babette.

In another example, one of our clients posted the following story in our private Facebook group:

Dear Noah,

My business is on pace to double this month. Prior to finding your program, I tried several home-based businesses, but my own limiting programming created a self-imposed barrier. I called it the fear of rejection, when it was really the fear of success. Simply put, I didn't think I deserved to succeed so I was actually repelling positive results. Only five weeks after starting your program, I've identified two serious business builders, and one of them has already enrolled their first customer. At this pace, I will develop a solid second income in the next few months. This is more than I accomplished with any other business in the last decade. Thank you, Noah.

One of the most inspiring quotes I've ever read on the subject of overcoming fear came from author Marianne Williamson in her book *A Return to Love*. She writes:

> Our deepest fear is not that we are inadequate. Our deepest fear is that we are powerful beyond measure. It is our light, not our darkness that most frightens us. We ask ourselves, "Who am I to be brilliant, gorgeous, talented, and fabulous?" Actually, who are you not to be? You are a child of God. Your playing small does not serve the world. There is nothing enlightened about shrinking so that other people won't feel insecure around you. We are born to make manifest the glory of God within us. It's not just in some of us; it's in everyone. And as we let our own light shine, we consciously give other people permission to do the same. As we are liberated from our own fear, our presence automatically liberates others.

Am I saying that when you use The Power Habits® System, you'll never feel fear again? Of course not; fear is a real human emotion that is there to protect you. What I am saying, however, is that following The Power Habits System will help you to take action, even in the face of fear.

Let's face it: it's perfectly natural to feel hurt when someone disapproves of you or rejects you. It's also totally natural to feel fear when you're thinking of trying something new. Complete the exercises in this chapter to help you find the courage to do that thing you're afraid of and take that action that will enable you to express more of Who You Really Are, because you'll find that on the other side of your fear lies the freedom you desire.

NOAH'S NOTES (IN A NUTSHELL)

1. Your level of success is determined by *driving forces* (the energy behind something in motion) and *restraining forces* (the energy that stops something in motion). Those two forces acting upon each other create a state of *equilibrium,* or your Current Perceived Reality.

2. That's why Power Habit #10 is **Claim Your Power**—because it means you're going to take action to increase your driving forces and decrease your restraining forces.

3. When I coach individuals, teams, or organizations, we often start with a *Force-Field Analysis,* which means identifying the driving forces and restraining forces at work to create your Current Perceived Reality.

4. One of the most powerful driving forces is the power of "I'll show you"—which is the internal drive to make other people wrong when they don't believe you can do something.

5. The most powerful restraining force is fear, because fear is the anticipation or expectation of pain. Since fear is an emotional reaction meant to keep us from harm, trying to pretend fear doesn't exist simply doesn't work.

6. While everyone feels fear, Unconsciously Successful People take action even in the face of fear. The good news is, you can do this too when you install The Power Habits® System in your life and business.

#POWERHABITSCHALLENGE #10

1. For your tenth Power Habits Challenge, write a post or share a video about why Claiming Your Power is crucial to your success, and include one thing you're going to do from this chapter this week, using the hashtag #PowerHabitsChallenge.

2. Be sure to tag me @NoahStJohn so I'll see your post.

CHAPTER 16

POWER HABIT #11: LIVE YOUR BECAUSE

"The secret to permanently breaking any bad habit is to love something greater than the habit."
— Bryant McGill

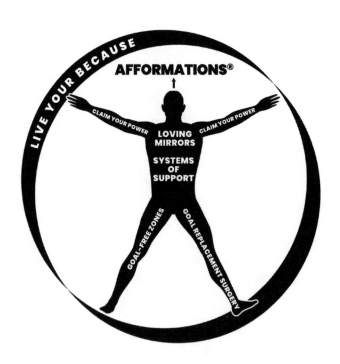

Aprofessional dancer must live with constant pain, often both physical and emotional. One night on stage during a performance of *Carmina Burana,* I was performing a lift—something I'd done hundreds of times in my career—when I heard and felt something go "pop" in my hip. At that moment, I knew it was the end of my professional dance career. I was 21 years old.

Because most professional dancers live in near-poverty—in my case, I had moved right in—I had no money, no business experience, no connections, and no idea what to do with the rest of my life. However, I had to find a way to make ends meet, so I worked a series of "survival jobs" and hated each one more than the last. By this time, I was also trying to find employment as an actor in television and movies, yet Hollywood was underwhelmed by my performances. Finally, at age 25, I had had enough and decided to kill myself.

I'm not exaggerating for effect. Because I had never known more than a few moments of happiness in my entire life and had spent most of my years being angry, broke, and miserable, I finally decided to commit suicide.

Except I didn't own a gun. Then I remembered something about how the exhaust from your car engine would kill you if you kept your car running in a closed garage. So I decided to do it that way.

Except I didn't have a garage, either. I was living in a tiny apartment, and my building only had open auto bays, which meant there was no way to trap the exhaust from my car. So I decided to drive around the neighborhood until I found an unlocked garage that I could pull my car in, shut the door behind me, and kill myself.

Wouldn't you know it: it took me only a few minutes of driving around until I found an empty garage with its door wide open. I saw that I could drive right in, shut the door behind me, close my eyes…and that would be that.

Staring at the reality of what I was about to do, I paused. *Think about what you're about to do,* a voice seemed to say to me. *Are you sure you want to do this?*

And then I saw it: the thing that saved my life.

> AT THAT MOMENT, I SAW THE THING THAT SAVED MY LIFE.

Parked in the corner of the garage was a child's bicycle. It had a white seat and those white things you hold on to at the ends of the handlebars. It looked just like a bike I'd had when I was a kid.

I thought, *Wait a minute. This isn't an abandoned home. A family must live here. What are they going to do when they come home and find my dead body in their garage?*

In my mind's eye, I pictured a woman coming home, finding my body, and screaming in shock and terror. I saw a man trying to comfort the woman, but her being inconsolable. I saw the bicycle's owner, a child, standing there not understanding what was happening, but knowing that something was terribly wrong. And I saw my horribly selfish act traumatizing this family for the rest of their lives.

I realized that I couldn't do this to them. Even though I didn't know who they were (and will never know), I recognized that what I was about to do wasn't fair to them, so I turned the car around and went home.

When I got home, I got in the shower—I guess I wanted to cleanse myself of that experience. As I stood there in the shower, I said out loud, "God, I don't know why You spared my life, but You did, so I promise to give the rest of my life to You."

Shortly thereafter, I decided to go back to college and major in religious studies so I could follow in the footsteps of Dr. Stephen R. Covey, whose book *The 7 Habits of Highly Effective People* helped me realize that I too wanted to help people find and fulfill their life's purpose.

And that's how I came to the two epiphanies that changed my life in 1997. The first epiphany was The Shower That Changed Everything, where I discovered Afformations®; the second was the seminar where I discovered *success anorexia* and birthed The Power Habits® System.

Yet something was still missing. I still didn't have the right Systems of Support, which led me to trust the wrong people and hire a bunch of "gurus" who took my money.

I WENT FROM BASEMENT TO BESTSELLER IN 24 MONTHS BY DOING THIS.

I also found myself in an abusive relationship that ended up costing me tens of thousands of dollars. Eventually, I ended that relationship, but by that time I was $40,000 in debt and was forced to move back into my parents' home (as you read about in the beginning of this book).

I felt embarrassed, ashamed, and like I'd let everybody down. But I finally realized that if I had created this life that I *didn't* want, I could also create one that I *did* want. (Isn't it amazing what happens when we apply our own teachings?)

Slowly but surely, momentum started to build. Word spread about my work again. More clients started to tell their friends, and those friends became clients themselves.

When money came in, I saved it. Less than six months after being forced to move into my parents' home, I had saved enough to get my own place. Within a year, I had paid off all of my debts and became 100 percent debt-free.

Within 24 months, I signed a six-figure book deal with one of the world's largest publishers and became a best-selling author for the first time. So I literally went from basement to bestseller in 24 months!

A short time later, a friend introduced me to this gorgeous blonde named Babette. Not long after that, I got up the courage to ask her to go ballroom dancing with me, because I figured if I could take her dancing, maybe I'd sweep her off her feet. It turns out that I was the one who got swept off my feet!

Today our days are filled with friends, family, laughter, and love. I have an amazing team that supports me and our wonderful clients in over 120 countries around the world. I'm privileged to do keynote speeches, lead private workshops, and host life-changing seminars and exclusive mastermind groups for amazing people just like you.

My books have now been published in 18 languages, and I'm always humbled to receive a postcard, letter, or post on social media from one of my loyal readers like you who tell me how my work changed their life—sometimes sent from halfway around the world!

The point of this story is to share with you how my life changed, and how your life can change, when you follow the 11th and final Power Habit. The 11th Power Habit is called **Live Your Because**.

WHAT DOES IT MEAN TO LIVE YOUR BECAUSE?

Unconsciously Successful People have mastered the habit of expressing their Authentic Self, living their life's purpose, and getting paid for the privilege of doing it. I call this *Living Your Because.* When you are Living Your Because, it's like going to heaven…without the inconvenience of dying! Because Living Your Because means you're expressing Who You Really Are and prospering from that expression, through the systematic process of adding value to other people's lives.

However, right now, millions of people don't know their life purpose or mission; they don't know why they're here on Earth. I know, because I used to be one of them. The problem is, when you don't know your mission or why you're here on Earth, it can lead to emotions ranging from depression, frustration, and stress, to anger, guilt, and despair. It can also lead to addictions like tobacco, alcohol, gambling, and the like.

That's why the habit of Living Your Because is so powerful—because it will empower you not just to "make a living," but to actually design and live the Freedom Lifestyle you truly desire.

LIVING YOUR BECAUSE IS LIKE GOING TO HEAVEN WITHOUT THE INCONVENIENCE OF DYING.

There is one inescapable truth when it comes to abundance and prosperity: people don't follow followers; people follow leaders. YOU can be that leader. However, in order to become that leader, you must develop the habit of Living Your Because.

HOW TO LIVE YOUR BECAUSE

The five essential steps to Live Your Because are:

Step 1: Discover What You're Great At.

Step 2: Determine Your Unique Offer.

Step 3: Decide on Your Target Market.

Step 4: Design Your Automatic Income Blueprint.

Step 5: Define Your Growth Strategy.

LIVE YOUR BECAUSE STEP 1: DISCOVER WHAT YOU'RE GREAT AT

You have skills, strengths, and things you love to do that can not just make you money, but also help you to Live Your Because. After coaching people just like you from around the world and helping them add more than $2.2 billion in sales, I've come to realize that the first step to Live Your Because is to make an honest assessment of your strengths, skills, and desires. That's why I call this first step *Discover What You're Great At.*

With my coaching clients, I usually have them start by answering these and other related questions:

1. I feel my strengths are:

2. I admire people who:

3. I'm really good at:

4. What I enjoy doing:

5. My favorite ways to express my skills and talents:

6. If money were no object, I would:

7. If I gave myself permission to pursue my dreams, I would:

LIVE YOUR BECAUSE STEP 2: DETERMINE YOUR UNIQUE OFFER

In the context of Living Your Because, I teach my clients that an *offer* is a package, product, program, or service that you sell to a specific target market or customer. Therefore, the next step of this process is to *Determine Your Unique Offer.*

Throughout this book, I've shared several unique offers that you can take advantage of, so you can accelerate your results and reach your goals faster and easier. Naturally, some people will choose to get "offended" when you make an offer—even if it's something they want!—because they'll see it as though you're trying to "sell" them something (oh, the horror!).

Yet here's the truth—three truths, actually:

Truth #1: The word *sell* comes from an Old English word meaning "to serve." (Look it up if you don't believe me.)

Truth #2: Nothing happens unless someone sells something.

Truth #3: People love to buy, but hate to be sold.

Therefore, if you choose to be "offended" when someone makes you an offer—whether in person, on the phone, at an event, or (ahem) in a book, here are three things I know about you:

Thing #1: You've got head trash about money, which means...

Thing #2: You're not making much money right now, which means...

Thing #3: This is the EXACT thing you need right now.

This is also why we spend so much time on the Inner Game and Outer Game of Money at my live seminars and private workshops—for the precise reason that so many people have head trash about money, which is keeping them from making the money they desire.

For now, you can start to Determine Your Unique Offer by answering these questions:

1. I'm good at giving people value by doing the following things:

2. I've helped people in the past by doing the following things:

3. How I currently serve my clients or customers:

4. How I'd like to serve my clients or customers in the future:

LIVE YOUR BECAUSE STEP 3:
DECIDE ON YOUR TARGET MARKET

Once you Discover What You're Great At and Determine Your Unique Offer, the next step is to *Decide on Your Target Market.* This is crucial, because when I ask my coaching clients who their target market is, many will say: "Everybody!"

(Facepalm emoji)

Okay, let's go over this one more time...

Yes, I understand that your offer is so wonderful, amazing, and fantastic that it could, in fact, help everybody. There's just one teensy problem: *How, exactly, are you going to reach "everybody"?*

As annoying as it is, and as counterintuitive as it seems, the more you try to reach "everybody," the more you will end up reaching "nobody." That's because marketing—i.e., the process of telling your target market about your offer and how it will benefit them—has become so vastly convoluted and overwhelmingly confusing that trying to reach everybody is the surest road to financial disaster and ruin.

Ironically, this is a corollary of Benjamin Franklin's old adage: "There are many roads to success, but only one sure road to failure; and that is to try to please everyone else."

In this context, I have updated wise ol' Ben's advice to this:

There are many roads to success, but only one sure road to failure; and that is to try and reach everyone with your message.

Therefore, begin to Decide on Your Target Market by answering these questions:

1. What group or groups of people do I really ENJOY serving?

2. What group or groups can I REACH easily?

3. What group or groups are GREAT in number?

4. What group or groups SPEND money on what I have to offer?

LIVE YOUR BECAUSE STEP 4: DESIGN YOUR AUTOMATIC INCOME BLUEPRINT

Over the last 20-plus years of mentoring entrepreneurs, teams, and organizations, I've seen that there is one major difference between individuals and companies that are growing and those that are not, and it can be expressed in the following four-word phrase:

PEOPLE FAIL. SYSTEMS SUCCEED.

Management expert W. Edwards Deming said it like this: "Put a good person in a bad system, and the system will win every time."

The point is that every person wants to succeed. We all want to win. So the problem is not one of lack of motivation, but lack of systems.

That's why I developed a system I call **The Automatic Income Blueprint**. *The Automatic Income Blueprint* is a set of interconnected steps that lead people from "I've never heard of you" to "I'd like to buy from you" to "I'm glad I bought from you" to "I'm telling all my friends about you."

For instance, think about a recent movie you saw that you really enjoyed. Before the movie came out, you had never heard of it. Then you watched a commercial, saw a trailer in the theater, or had a friend tell you about it. Then you went to see the movie. And now you recommend it to your friends because you enjoyed it so much.

THE PROBLEM ISN'T LACK OF MOTIVATION, BUT LACK OF SYSTEMS.

273

Well, the same could be said about essentially anything you buy—and anything that other people will buy from you.

The point is, struggling entrepreneurs don't have a system or process in place to make this happen—they're just crossing their fingers and *hoping* it happens.

Ironically, it's actually easier and cheaper to put the systems in place than NOT have to them—because right now, the entire thing depends on YOUR effort and energy, and that is a sure path to burnout.

That's why I help entrepreneurs and companies to Design Your Automatic Income Blueprint—because, while it's a simple concept, it can be tricky to put in place. However, once it's in place, you'll wish you had done it years ago, because of all the savings of time, money, and effort.

To begin to Design Your Automatic Income Blueprint, answer these questions:

1. What's the first thing my clients or customers usually buy from me?

2. What's the first thing my clients or customers SHOULD buy from me?

3. What's the NEXT thing they should buy from me? And the thing after that?

4. What's the first thing I need to do to have an Automatic Income Blueprint in place in my business?

LIVE YOUR BECAUSE STEP 5: DEFINE YOUR GROWTH STRATEGY

As you begin to move up the ladder of success, life will throw things at you that you could never anticipate. It's happened to me, it's happened to every Unconsciously Successful Person, and it will happen to you too.

That's why the final step to Live Your Because is to *Define Your Growth Strategy*—because when you do this step, you'll transcend "positive thinking" and "motivation" and begin to **make your success AUTOMATIC**. (This is one reason why the motto of SuccessClinic.com is **"Making Success Automatic® Since 1997."**)

If you don't know your Growth Strategy yet, you'll need to get one fast—because if you don't, there's a strong chance you'll give up and abandon your dreams when things get tough. This is also why so many people who start out with a dream to help people end up quitting because they simply couldn't keep going through the rough patches.

I'm not trying to be all doom and gloom here. All I'm saying is that life is full of unexpected surprises. (That's why they call them "surprises" and not "expecteds.")

When things get tough, does that mean you should keep going in that direction, or should you go in a new direction? When you're coming up against one roadblock after another, does it mean you're on the wrong road?

The answer is, there's no one answer. Sometimes things are toughest right before your biggest breakthrough, and sometimes it's a sign that it's time to go in a new direction.

That's another reason to get the input of a coach or mentor—to give you that perspective you need to make the right

AT SUCCESSCLINIC.COM HAS BEEN MAKING SUCCESS AUTOMATIC® SINCE 1997.

decisions for you. The right mentor will believe in you, yet will also be truthful and honest enough to tell you when you should probably take a different road—or if you're on the right road, and just need to make a few adjustments in order to reach your New Desired Reality.

That's why it's important to choose the right coach or mentor to give you the proper perspective while ultimately empowering you to make the best decisions for you and your family.

To begin to Define Your Growth Strategy, answer these questions:

1. How am I currently getting new customers?

2. What is the average amount that a customer buys from me on the first purchase (Average Order Value)?

3. What is the average amount that a customer buys from me over the lifetime of that customer (Lifetime Customer Value)?

4. What's the first thing I can do to increase my Average Order Value and Lifetime Customer Value so I can make more money and serve more people?

THESE TWO SENTENCES DESCRIBE ALL HUMAN EMOTION

I was meditating one morning when I realized that all human emotion can be described in two simple sentences. I know it sounds crazy, but once I saw them in my mind's eye, I realized that these two sentences— so simple and yet so elegant—encompass the entire range of human emotion. In addition, they explain how to fix any negative emotion we might experience.

Ready?

Here are the two sentences that describe all human emotion:

WHEN YOUR OPINION OF YOUR PAST, PRESENT, AND FUTURE TENDS TO BE POSITIVE, YOU WILL BE HAPPY.

WHEN YOUR OPINION OF YOUR PAST, PRESENT, OR FUTURE TENDS TO BE NEGATIVE, YOU WILL BE UNHAPPY.

Those two sentences describe all human emotion.

What is the key word in both of those sentences? *Opinion.* Why?

Because it's not what happens to us; it's *our opinion* of what happens to us that determines our thoughts, feelings, and habits—and all of those together form our very lives.

For instance, do you know someone who's carrying around a negative opinion of their *past*—something that happened to them 10, 20, or 40 years ago?

Do you know someone who's carrying around a negative opinion of their *present*—not appreciating the gifts they have right now?

And do you know someone who's carrying around a negative opinion of their *future*—perhaps being afraid of something that hasn't even happened yet?

And do you know this person, let's say...*intimately?*

Conversely, think of someone you know who is happy. I'll bet you dollars to donuts (not that I want donuts; I have no idea what that phrase means) that that happy person has a *positive opinion* of their past, present, AND their future.

Notice that your opinion of your past, present, and future is, in fact, your life. Indeed, I argue that *your life is nothing more or less than **your opinion** of your past, your present, and your future.*

Your past exists only in your mind. Nowhere else in the entire universe does your past exist, except in the squishy seven-pound organ between your ears.

Your present exists only in your mind. Even if you live with 12 other people, no one else on Earth experiences your present, except you.

Your future exists only in your mind. Your hopes, dreams, fears, desires—all there in your lovely brain.

Therefore, if you want to do what I've been talking about throughout this book and start to get real results in your life and business, you need to start by doing these three things:

Step 1: Forgive your past.

Step 2: Appreciate your present.

Step 3: Step into your best future.

Many people believe they've missed opportunities in the past and that's why they're unhappy. For example, do you know someone who says, "I'll never be successful because I never finished college," or "I can't win because I didn't get that promotion," or some other excuse?

They're holding on to the past to explain why they're not successful in the present and telling themselves they'll never succeed in the future.

START APPRECIATING YOUR LIFE AND STOP DEPRECIATING IT.

Similarly, many people fail to appreciate what they have right now, in the present. The word *appreciate* literally means "to raise in value." What are most people doing? Right—the exact opposite.

Instead of appreciating what they have, they're *depreciating* what they have. They're constantly saying things like "Why don't I have all the things so-and-so has? Why don't I have as much money as so-and-so has?" Of course, social media only exacerbates this problem by serving up a never-ending stream of "Look how cool and happy I am" images of other people (and their smiling, laughing perfect family) and how amazing their (highlight reel) lives are.

Of course, we need goals and things we're striving for. The problem is when nothing is ever good enough for you, and this happens when you don't actively appreciate your present.

And of course, many people fear the future. With the constant drumbeat of doom and gloom from the media, it's no wonder that suicide rates are up in the United States from just a few years ago. I believe this is just another symptom of the fact that people don't believe they can live the life they imagined.

HOW TO STEP INTO YOUR BEST FUTURE

Right now, you desire to live a better life. Otherwise, you would not still be reading this book. Yet many people are so weighed down by disempowering beliefs about their past and present that they can't see how to live a better future.

That's why I want you to write what happens in your Perfect Average Day. Think about your average day that you live right now. Your alarm clock goes off. You get out of bed. You eat breakfast (or not). Maybe the kids are running around, getting ready for school.

You go to work. Are you doing work you love? Do you work out of your home, or do you travel to your office?

You go through your day at work. Are you excited or bored, happy or frustrated, feeling a sense of significance and contribution, or something else entirely? Are you working with people whom you like and who like you, or would you cross to the other side of the street if you saw them walking toward you? Does the day go by fast, or are you watching the clock until quitting time?

You come home. Are you feeling tired and worn out—or satisfied with a job well done?

You go to bed. What are the last thoughts you think before drifting off to sleep? Contentment, gratitude, appreciation—or dread at the thought of having to do it all over again tomorrow?

Do you see what I'm getting at? *This is how we live our lives.*

And before you know it, a year's gone by...two years... five years...ten years...twenty years...and more. Yet you're still saying to yourself, "Someday I'll..."

STEP INTO YOUR BEST FUTURE BY STARTING WHERE YOU ARE RIGHT NOW.

Have you ever noticed there are no trips to "Someday Isle"? The fact is, you either take ACTION to do the thing, or else it never happens.

That's why I'm encouraging you to stop thinking about going to Someday Isle and instead start taking ACTION to make your Freedom Lifestyle a reality. Start by answering these questions about your Perfect Average Day:

1. How do I start my Perfect Average Day?

2. Where am I?

3. Who am I with?

4. Who are my clients or customers?

5. What do I do during the day?

6. What do I have for my meals?

7. What do I do for fun?

8. What do I want to do to leave a legacy for my family and for the world?

9. What's the first thing I'm going to do right now to make my Perfect Average Day a reality?

To Live Your Because means to express and enjoy the highest levels of success, happiness, and fulfillment—because as you develop the habit of expressing Who You Really Are, you're also going to install Systems that will allow you and your family to prosper as you provide more value to others.

That's why, when you install this final Power Habit of Unconsciously Successful People, you're going to stop apologizing for Who You Really Are and give yourself *Permission to Succeed*® at the highest levels imaginable.

NOAH'S NOTES (IN A NUTSHELL)

1. Unconsciously Successful People have mastered the habit of expressing their Authentic Self, living their life's purpose, and getting paid for the privilege of doing it.

2. That's why Power Habit #11 is **Live Your Because,** because it means you're going to install Systems so you can finally prosper from expressing Who You Really Are and adding value to other people's lives.

3. The five essential steps to Live Your Because are:

   a. Discover What You're Great At.

   b. Determine Your Unique Offer.

   c. Decide on Your Target Market.

   d. Design Your Automatic Income Blueprint.

   e. Define Your Growth Strategy.

4. The two sentences that describe all human emotion are:

   a. *When your opinion of your past, present, and future tends to be positive, you will be happy.*

   b. *When your opinion of your past, present, or future tends to be negative, you will be unhappy.*

5. The key word in both of those sentences is opinion—because it's not what happens to us, but our opinion of what happens to us, that determines our quality of life.

6. If you want to get better results in your life, health, relationships, or business, start by doing these three things:

   a. Forgive your past.

   b. Appreciate your present.

   c. Step into your best future.

7. If you want to hire me to coach you, so YOU too can step into your best future and Live Your Because without having to work harder (and without Information Overload or "tech overwhelm"), book a time for us to talk at **www.WorkingwithNoah.com**

#POWERHABITSCHALLENGE #11

1. For your eleventh Power Habits Challenge, write a post or share a video on social media about why Living Your Because is so important to your success, and one thing you're going to do from this chapter this week, using the hashtag **#PowerHabitsChallenge.**

2. Be sure to tag me **@NoahStJohn** so I'll see your post.

PART 3

NEXT STEPS

CHAPTER 17

YOUR BEST NEXT STEP

"If breaking a habit has been hard for you to do,
then a helping hand is in order."
— Kenneth Schwarz

As we come to the conclusion of this book, the spirit that fills the hearts and minds of the people who brought you this is one of *reverence*—reverence for the principles we've discussed, reverence for the program itself, and reverence for the amazing people like you who have shared their experiences with us.

Now that you've been exposed to The Power Habits® System, I'd like to issue you a simple challenge: if you've been driving down the road of life with one foot on the brake, I've given you some simple tools and strategies that can empower you to reach your goals faster and easier than ever before.

However, even the best hammer in the world won't help you build your house if you never pick it up and use it.

That's because if you want to live the Freedom Lifestyle of your dreams, you must, by definition, expand your Familiar Zone. That means right now, you have two options:

Option 1: Take everything you've just learned and try to do it all on your own.

Yes, it will take longer and you might even make some painful, costly mistakes if you choose this option. However, you can do it this way—and in fact, that's what the average person will do, because it appears to be the "easier" choice.

However, there is a smarter choice—the one that smart, savvy people like you take to speed their progress toward success and victory, and that is:

Option 2: Move faster with me and my team so you don't have to do it alone anymore.

Why go at it alone when I've done all the heavy lifting for you? Why not give yourself the gift of peace of mind, happiness, and fulfillment without having to work so hard?

The truth is, you don't have to reinvent the wheel—because my proven strategies and methods have been tried and tested by more than 100,000 successful people just like you from around the world, which means they're proven to work.

YOU'RE GOING TO BE HAPPIER AND A LOT MORE SUCCESSFUL WHEN YOU CHOOSE THIS OPTION.

That's why my team and I are inviting you to join us in **our Platinum and VIP Coaching programs.**

Why? Because my radically simple system will work for you, even if you have...

✓ A super-busy schedule (this is lifestyle friendly!)

✓ Tried a bunch of other things in the past

✓ Low self-esteem or your self-confidence has been shot

✓ People in your life who don't believe you can achieve your dreams, or

✓ Even if you THINK you've tried everything already.

Because I'll give you my proven, research-backed business and performance coaching strategies that have produced more than $2.2 billion in sales for me and my clients.

HERE'S WHAT THIS WILL DO FOR YOU

When it comes to making more money, many entrepreneurs are drowning in Information Overload, which creates "paralysis by analysis" and means you're either not taking action or not getting the results you truly desire.

That's why my Power Habits® Certified Coaches and I will help you quickly get out of Information Overload, so you can rapidly start making more money without having to work so hard.

You will completely understand how to get out of your own way—without having to use willpower or "psych yourself up." As a result, you will unlock your hidden power to succeed in wealth, health, relationships, and your family life.

In addition, you'll also stop procrastinating and cure "Shiny Object Syndrome," which means you'll finally be able to finish that project that's been sitting on your desk (or in your head) forever—and that means you'll be able to attract a lot more money into your life, so you'll have more confidence to do the things you really desire to do.

And that means you'll have a greater impact so you can transform lives around the world and leave a legacy of goodness and happiness for your children and the greater community. That's why this program is for you if…

✓ You're frustrated by not having the income and happiness you want.

✓ You want step-by-step guidance to get from where you are to where you want to be.

✓ You've ever felt frustrated because you're not where you want to be in life or business.

✓ You want to get rid of your head trash and stop holding yourself back.

✓ You desire to get more out of every investment you'll make for the rest of your life.

Plus, when you work with us at SuccessClinic.com, you're a student, not just a "customer." That's because (and I know this sounds old-fashioned) we genuinely CARE about you and your success. Plus, I'm on a mission to change our industry for the better, because I'm tired of all the sleazy marketers and "gurus" who are great at marketing, but who can't teach their way out of a paper bag!

That means that not only will we be working together in this program; you'll also get to take advantage of our Heroic Customer Support that's become our hallmark. You'll get your questions answered, you'll never feel alone, and you'll get the "Star Treatment" for which we've become famous.

REMEMBER THE ZIP LINE?

Remember the zip line story I told you at the beginning of this book?

Whenever you're presented with an opportunity to make a quantum leap in your life or business—to get better results without having to work so hard—you have those same three options I faced at the top of that mountain:

Option 1: Try to go back to the way things were. (Sadly, this isn't possible.)

Option 2: Try to stay right where you are. (This isn't actually possible, either.)

Option 3: Take ACTION even in the face of fear.

Of course it's scary—trying any new thing always is. Yet have you ever noticed that when lots and lots of other people have tried something and gotten great results, there's a great chance it will work for you too? (And if you don't believe it, that's your head trash talking. How much longer are you going to let your Negative Reflection boss you around?)

And, just like my zip line story, when you take that first step toward your new, happier, more successful lifestyle, my team and I will be right here to catch you and give you the VIP Treatment you deserve!

ONE MORE (EMBARRASSING) FACT

Let me conclude by sharing this rather embarrassing fact about myself with you: *I never intended to be an entrepreneur.* It's true: my first attempts to build my business were dismal failures. I assumed that I just didn't have what it takes to succeed, that I didn't have the skills, and that it just wasn't meant to be.

I ended up spending over $500,000 on "gurus" and so-called "experts" who took my money, yet couldn't teach their way out of a paper bag. That's why I vowed to create the easiest, fastest, most effective programs on the planet to help people around the world to get results, no matter their age, background, or self-imposed limitations. And in so doing, create a company that wasn't just about making a profit; but more importantly, about transforming lives.

After I finally succeeded, I stumbled on my Formula quite by accident. The truth is, I just was looking for a way to pay my bills and get out from under the sucking crush of credit card debt. Yet once that took off, I made millions.

THIS ISN'T JUST ABOUT MAKING A PROFIT. IT'S ABOUT TRANSFORMING LIVES.

Today I've been blessed to teach these methods to thousands and thousands of people just like you—my coaching clients and mastermind students who are making millions and millions of dollars themselves.

Despite my lack of natural talent, I became the most sought-after mentor of how to get rid of your head trash and achieve Inner Game Mastery in the industry. It's through that experience of "failure" that I learned a very simple lesson that I want to share with you: *talent cannot out-perform a formula.*

It's true: talent and hard work alone are NOT enough to create true, lasting success. However, simply following my Formula has empowered people just like you from around the world to duplicate, and even surpass, my own financial success. And now it's your turn...

ONE FINAL GUARANTEE

More than 200 years ago, Benjamin Franklin wrote: "There are only two guarantees in life: death and taxes." With all due respect to ol' Ben, I argue that there is a third guarantee in life, and it's this:

If you choose to do nothing, nothing will change. As you know, the definition of insanity is "doing the same thing and expecting different results." Therefore, the third guarantee is that if you keep doing what you're doing, you'll keep getting what you're getting.

Yes, it takes ACTION. Yes, it takes COMMITMENT.

However, if you're not where you want to be in life, if you want to go from where you are to where you want to be and finally get rid of the head trash that's been holding you back, you owe it to yourself to take this one simple step, so you can begin to live the Freedom Lifestyle of your dreams.

HERE'S WHAT TO DO NOW

If you want to reach your life and business goals up to 300% faster without having to work harder, "psych yourself up" or even use willpower...

Join Power Habits® Academy now.

Because in this legendary program, you will discover how to use our proven methods that have created more than $2.2 billion in added revenues for impact-driven entrepreneurs, salespeople, service providers and business professionals just like you from around the world.

That's because we show you how to do consciously what highly successful people do unconsciously---in ways that the "gurus" and "Naturals" never could.

In fact, Power Habits® Academy is specifically designed for the entrepreneur, sales professional, or service provider who's looking for the perfect combination of strategy, accountability, and peer support— all on a foundation of attention to spiritual development and continued personal growth.

Join Power Habits® Academy now at:

PowerHabitsAcademy.com/go

CHAPTER 18

YOU'RE INVITED

"Sow a thought, and you reap an act;
Sow an act, and you reap a habit;
Sow a habit, and you reap a character;
Sow a character, and you reap a destiny."
— *Ralph Waldo Emerson*

Did you know that in less than 90 days from now you could be living a richer, happier life while working LESS than you are right now?

How do I know? Because I regularly help busy people just like you to double their business (or more), sometimes in just a matter of months, or even *weeks.* And since you've already read many of their success stories in this book, now it's YOUR turn to win!

YOU'RE INVITED TO FREEDOM LIFESTYLE EXPERIENCE

Freedom Lifestyle Experience iis the world's premiere event for impact-driven entrepreneurs, sales professionals, and service providers who want to live your "Dream Lifestyle" without Information Overload and without having to sacrifice Who You Really Are.

As your mentor and guide, I will walk you through every step and show you exactly what to do to experience the success you're seeking. And unlike other programs that leave you frustrated, confused, and feeling like you're missing something, I will teach you my proven, step-by-step skills, strategies, and tools required to master the Inner Game and Outer Game of Success.

And once you understand these strategies and begin to apply them, get ready to see massive improvement in your sales, your business, and your lifestyle.

HERE'S WHAT THIS WILL DO FOR YOU

It's the entrepreneur's dream: traveling the world, making money while you're relaxing on the beach, balancing parenthood and business so you still have time to catch your kids' soccer games and dance recitals...while bringing in a handsome income to support your lifestyle and family.

Yet for too many people, that dream has turned into a nightmare, because instead of working where you want and when you want, you're slaving away day and night (including weekends). Which means now you're working for your business, instead of having your business working hard for YOU.

Well, all that's about to change, because here's just a small taste of what you'll get at when you join us:

- ✓ The right way to quickly and easily attract more money without "tech overwhelm" so you can spend 90% of your time doing what you LOVE.

- ✓ How to stop stepping over thousands of dollars every time you step in the office.

✓ How to transform your annual income into your monthly income without having to "hustle" or work like a dog.

✓ How to stop working so hard for your business, and start having your business work hard for YOU.

✓ How small adjustments will equal big results for you.

STOP WORKING SO HARD FOR YOUR BUSINESS AND START HAVING YOUR BUSINESS WORK HARD FOR YOU!

✓ You will save an enormous amount of time, energy, effort & wasted money.

✓ People will magnetically attract to you, so you can grow and scale at will.

✓ You will avoid the #1 mistake everyone makes that causes people to say "no" to you.

✓ How to stop being the "best-kept secret" so you never have to hear that phrase again!

✓ How to ethically get anyone, anytime, anyplace to LOVE YOU and want to do business with you.

✓ My proven method to eliminate 80% of your stress in less than 10 minutes a day.

✓ Exactly what to do when faced with frustration or rejection. Do this right and you will become *fundamentally unstoppable.*

✓ And so much more…

BRING A FRIEND FOR FREE

Imagine having a trusted friend, colleague, or partner there to share the transformation you'll get at this event, so you and those closest to you can level up in all areas of your lives.

Imagine what could be possible if you created your own team of unstoppable support, creativity, and inspiration, so you can consciously create relationships that fuel your success and fulfillment.

FACT: There's nothing more powerful than a community of connected minds, which is why we are taking the extra step to make it possible, so you can share all these benefits with a friend.

And because you purchased this book, when you claim YOUR ticket, you can also bring a friend for FREE.

Claim your "Buy 1, Bring a Friend <u>FREE</u>" tickets now at:

FreedomLifeX.com

RECOMMENDED RESOURCES

THE IDEAL PROFESSIONAL SPEAKER
FOR YOUR NEXT CONFERENCE OR EVENT

Unify your team • Get out of overwhelm • Grow your business

Planning a successful conference or meeting is a huge job and responsibility. **That's why I want to make <u>YOUR</u> job easier!**

After delivering 1,000+ presentations, I can assure you that you can RELAX, knowing that you are working with a professional. That's because my #1 goal is to make **<u>YOU</u>** look great and have **<u>YOUR</u>** audience **<u>THANKING YOU</u>** for inviting me to speak for them.

Your audience will be instantly and highly ENGAGED, and they will leave INSPIRED and MOTIVATED to *"Overcome Obstacles and Achieve Greater Success!"*

Thank you for your consideration, and I look forward to working together to help **<u>YOU</u>** create **<u>YOUR BEST</u>** event **<u>EVER!</u>**

— Noah St. John

NOAH'S MOST REQUESTED TOPICS

The Power Habits® for Ultimate Success (Success / Peak Performance)

*Ideal for opening your event!

This keynote will help you...

✓ **Increase Productivity**

✓ **Remove Blocks to Success**

✓ **Drive Performance**

This motivational, humorous and high-energy message is ideal for an opening or closing session, because it is sure to **Refuel, Recharge and Reenergize your audience,** while helping them bridge the gap between daily habits and success.

Whether you are dealing with prospects, customers, associates, clients, employees, employers, family members, relationships, or personal issues, you CAN start using The Power Habits® for Ultimate Success!

Book Noah for your next event at

BookNoah.com

The Power Habits® of Legendary Leadership
(Leadership / Teamwork / Team Building)

This keynote will help you...

✓ **Improve Leadership from the Inside Out**

✓ **Get 1–3 Hours Back in Your Day**

✓ **Have More Time, More Energy,**
  Better Relationships, and More Money

This motivational leadership message will empower YOUR audience to motivate and inspire others to *outperform, outsell, and outhustle your competition!*

In this highly engaging talk, your audience will discover how to gain focus in a world of infinite distractions, and how to attract more opportunities and improve teamwork faster than they ever thought possible!

The Power Habits® to Supercharge Sales
(Sales / Peak Performance / Overcoming Adversity)

This keynote will help you...

✓ **Stimulate New Ideas**

✓ **Accelerate Growth**

✓ **Promote Teamwork**

This program is ideal for commissioned salespeople, business leaders, direct sales associates or independent professionals.

This empowering message is ideal for any sales-focused group as it is sure to ***ignite your sales audience*** while providing "real-world" sales strategies for attracting an abundance of sales!

Book Noah for your next event at

BookNoah.com

The Automatic Income Formula:
"How to Build Your 24/7 Automated Selling Machine"
(*Special for Entrepreneur Audiences*)

Is your business on the "Revenue Roller Coaster?" If you don't automate your sales process, you'll never have the one thing every business owner wants: ***predictable, profitable sales.***

Leveraging his 20-plus years of experience owning one of the world's original personal development websites, Noah will teach you how to reprogram your mind and set your business up for entrepreneurial success and accelerated achievement!

Book Noah for your next event at

BookNoah.com

"All I heard was great feedback! Thank you, Noah, for really engaging the audience. I am recommending you as a speaker for more chapter meetings."

—**Heather Gortz,** Meeting Planners International

"Noah is definitely NOT your typical motivational speaker! SIMPLY PHENOMENAL—A MUST-HAVE RESOURCE for your organization!"

—**Carol Stoops,** Senior National Sales Director, Mary Kay

"Noah St. John is the smartest, most effective seminar leader/trainer I've ever come across. Noah will not only get your people motivated, he'll give them the step-by-step tools to produce RESULTS!"

—**Casandra Hart,** Isagenix

"Noah St. John is a fantastic, highly engaging speaker! I highly encourage you to book Noah for YOUR next event, because he'll make YOU look like a ROCKSTAR!"

— Donna Marie Serritella, President of Direct Selling Solutions

"I highly recommend Noah St. John as a keynote speaker, because he's not only different from other speakers, he also really cares about his clients and resonates on a deep emotional level with his audience. **He's dynamic, impactful, inspiring, motivating, and professional— in short, the PERFECT speaker!**

—**Lauren Ashley Kay,** Meeting Planner, City Summit & Gala

Book Noah for your next event at BookNoah.com

BOOK A PRIVATE WORKSHOP

Are you leaving money on the table because you're overwhelmed with an endless to-do list and constant distractions?

What you need is simplicity, not more to-do's. That's why when you book a Private Workshop with Power Habits® author Noah St. John, you'll reach your business goals faster, easier, and with far less effort.

Using Noah's proven Power Habits® System, you'll implement high-level tactics and strategies that remove the hidden blocks to success. When you get your foot off the brake, rapid growth becomes a foregone conclusion.

PRIVATE WORKSHOPS ARE IDEAL IF:

✓ You're tired of working hard and not seeing the results you want.

✓ You're having trouble getting everyone on the same page.

✓ You're overwhelmed with all the choices out there.

✓ You're going it alone and longing for a second set of eyes on your systems and strategies.

✓ You're struggling with revenue month to month despite having a solid product or service.

THE BENEFITS
GO FAR BEYOND THE WORKSHOP

We'll listen to your challenges and opportunities. We'll work together to identify and eliminate what may be holding you back. Then, we'll provide fresh insights to get out of overwhelm and grow your business.

Something magical happens in the room every time we do this.

You'll see it too. The breakthroughs happen before your eyes. You'll get to the heart of your issues and smile as your team finally gels around a common goal.

Suddenly, all those to-do's won't feel like a chore anymore. You'll be excited to dig in, and the execution will feel easier than ever.

Best of all, you'll see the results in your revenue. Overwhelm will become simplified, frustration will turn into ease, and your business will finally break through that plateau that once felt impossible.

HERE'S WHAT THIS WILL DO FOR YOU:

- ✓ More focus and greater clarity to achieve important goals
- ✓ Clear and simple steps that lead to more opportunities
- ✓ A unified team that accomplishes more in less time
- ✓ Positive, successful communication among team members
- ✓ Less stress due to overwork
- ✓ Increased speed to market with new products and offers
- ✓ More team engagement as staffers see how their company improves the lives of customers
- ✓ A substantial return on their workshop investment as better habits translate into more sales and rapid growth

WITH A PRIVATE WORKSHOP YOU GET:

✓ A thorough understanding of The Power Habits® System

✓ Clarity on your growth strategy and a simple process to execute it

✓ The confidence these strategies will work for your company (no more second-guessing yourself)

✓ Actionable changes you can make immediately to improve team engagement

✓ A common language so your team will be more effective in sales and marketing

✓ A time-saving framework that will simplify how your team tackles future projects

✓ A simple company message that will unify your team around a single, meaningful mission.

"Refreshing and insightful. Noah gave tangible concepts that made me feel less crazy and re-instilled hope in my mind."

—Eden Silver, Dittman Incentive Marketing

"After using Noah's methods, I built the largest infill development company in Nashville with over $40 million in sales."

—Britnie Turner Keane, Founder and CEO of Aerial Development Group

Book a Private Workshop at NoahStJohn.com/private-workshop or call (330) 871-4331

ADDITIONAL PROGRAMS FROM NOAH ST. JOHN

Power Habits® Coach Network—Become a Noah St. John Power Habits® Certified Coach

Strategic Consulting for Business and Personal Growth

Quantity Discounts and Reader's Guides for Noah St. John Books

Product Licensing for Groups and Organizations

Visit NoahStJohn.com or call 1-330-871-4331 for more information on these and other programs.

Special <u>FREE</u> Bonus Gift for You

To help you achieve more success, there are **FREE BONUS RESOURCES** for you at:

FreeGiftFromNoah.com

- Exclusive training videos on how top achievers attract more opportunities, achieve more goals, and create more abundance

- Downloadable audio training on how to rewire your brain using Noah's AFFORMATIONS® Method

MOTIVATE AND INSPIRE OTHERS!

"SHARE THIS BOOK"
RETAIL $24.95

Special Quantity Discounts Available

To Place an Order, Contact:

(330) 871-4331
NoahStJohn.com

ACKNOWLEDGMENTS

My Most Grateful Thanks to…

God, the answer to all of our questions.

My beautiful wife Babette, for being my best friend and the best Loving Mirror I've ever had. Thank you for believing in me and supporting me, and for your tireless commitment to help me put a dent in the universe.

My parents, who sacrificed and gave more than they had.

My mother-in-law, Emily; my twin stepdaughters, Amber and Bambi, and stepson, Cody, for being outstanding examples of love and support.

Jack Canfield, for grokking my message when it was a bunch of pages bound with a piece of tape.

Dr. Stephen R. Covey, who inspired me to get into the business of helping people when the cassette album of *The 7 Habits of Highly Effective People* fell off a church bookshelf and landed at my feet. I swear I'm not making that up.

David Wildasin of Sound Wisdom and Vic Conant of Nightingale-Conant for seeing the vision of this book and my Power Habits® Series.

Through the years, many have shared ideas, inspiration, mentoring and support that have impacted my life, each in a different way. While it's impossible to thank everyone, please know that I appreciate you greatly:

Alex Mandossian, Arianna Huffington, Barbara DeAngelis, Ben Affleck, Bradley Cooper, Britney Spears, Chalene Johnson,

Dr. Daniel Amen, Derek Hough, Ellen Degeneres, Eric Worre, Gary Vaynerchuk, Gordon Ramsay, Halle Berry, Jay Abraham, Jenny McCarthy, Joel Osteen, John Lee Dumas, Lewis Howes, Marie Forleo, Marie Osmond, Mario Lopez, Dr. Mehmet Oz, Neil Strauss, Oprah Winfrey, Penn & Teller, Reba McEntire, Rita Rudner, Robin Leach, Ryan Seacrest, Suze Orman, Tai Lopez, Adam Farfan, Al Bala, Al Harris, Allison Maslan, Amanda Dobson, Andrew Lock, Andy Jenkins, Angel Fletcher, Anik Singal, Antoine Chevalier, Austin Zulauf, Bari Baumgardner, Berny Dohrmann, Bill and Steve Harrison, Bill Walsh, Billy Baldwin, Dr. Bob Hoffman, Dr. Brad Nelson, Brandon Boyd, Brian Clapp, Britnie Turner Keane, Bryan Bowman, Candace Sandy, Carolyn McCorkle, Chanida Nat Puranaputra, Chris Daigle, Chris Farrell, Chris Stoikos, Christy Dreiling, Cindy Villareal, Cody Sias, Courtney Epps, Craig Duswalt, Cynthia Kersey, Dan Bova, Dan Kuschell, Daniel Marcos, Dave Crenshaw, Dave Lindahl, Dave Meltzer, David Deutsch, David Osmond, DeAnna Rogers, Donna Johnson, Donna Marie Serritella, Donny Osmond, Erik Swanson, Dr. Fabrizio Mancini, Gail Gonzales, Gail Kingsbury, Garrett and Sylvia McGrath, George Gonzales, Glenn Morshower, Harvey Mackay, James Malinchak, Jason Hewlett, Jeff Altgilbers, Jeff Magee, Jen Groover, Jen Porro, Jessica and Rob Hefley, Jessica Meiczinger, Jim Kwik, JJ Virgin, Joe Polish, Joe Sugarman, Joe Vitale, Joey Davenport, John Assaraf, Dr. John Gray, John Feudo, John Redmond, John Shin, Jon Benson, Jonathan Fields, Jordan Stuart, Josh Felber, Justin Grant, Kara Codio, Karen Reilley, Keith Ungar, Ken and Kerri Courtright, Kimanzi Constable, Kody Bateman, Laura and Jerry Jacobs, Lauren Ashley Kay, Leslie Kyle Armstrong, Lisa Grossman, Lisa Nichols, Lisa Sasevich, Loral Langmeier, Luminita Sauvic, Mari Smith, Mary Glorfield, MaryEllen Tribby, Matthew Coleman, Megan Denhardt, Melissa Smith Eickenhorst, Mike Filsaime, Nathan Osmond, Neale Donald Walsch, Nick Kho, Paige O'Hara, Patrick Gentempo, Patty Aubrey, Patty Neger, Peter Shankman, Ray and Jessica Higdon, Reid Tracy, Rhonda Shaw, Richard Rossi, Rick Frishman, Roger Salam, Roland Frasier, Russell Brunson, Ryan Deiss, Ryan Holiday, Ryan Long, Sam Beard,

Sandra and Kym Yancey, Dr. Scot Gray, Scott and Rochelle Warren, Shanda Sumpter, Sharon Lechter, Sherrie Sokolowski, Spike Humer, Storey Pryor, Taylor Worre, Drs. Ted and Tom Morter, Temple Hayes, Tiffany Peterson, Todd Durkin, Tom and Adrian Chenault, Walter O'Brien, Verne Harnish, Yanik Silver and SO many other people who have helped me in my career!

Charles Duhigg, who deserves special recognition for his influence on my understanding of The Habit Loop.

Will Smith, for your music and for living a life that has inspired me to charge full steam at whatever I'm most afraid of.

Very special thanks to the vast and growing tribe of our phenomenal VIP Coaching Clients, Mastermind Family Members, and Power Habits® Certified Coaches around the world who believe in the power of this message. Thank you for spreading the word about our work to all corners of the globe!

Every day, as I hear more and more stories of how the coaching and mentorship work we do together is changing lives, you inspire, encourage, and uplift me. I am humbled by your stories of how my work has changed your lives—truly, more than you know.

Whether you're a member of our Platinum or VIP Coaching Family, attend one of our live events or online trainings this year, or simply commit to telling your friends about this book, I'm grateful for **YOU**— because every day brings with it the opportunity to be reborn in the next greatest version of ourselves.

Now it's <u>YOUR</u> turn—I look forward to being a part of <u>YOUR</u> Success Story!

INDEX

Z

ABOUT THE AUTHOR

NOAH ST. JOHN is an international keynote speaker, business and performance coach, and bestselling author who's famous for helping entrepreneurs make money: Since 1997, his coaching clients have added more than $2.2 billion in sales. His sought-after advice is known as the "secret sauce" to business and personal growth.

A highly in-demand keynote speaker, Noah's engaging and down-to-earth speaking style always gets high marks from audiences. Meeting planners say Noah St. John is **"A BIG draw," "The PERFECT Speaker,"** and **"A MUST-HAVE RESOURCE for every organization!"**

He is the only author in history to have works published by Hay House, HarperCollins, Simon & Schuster, Mindvalley, Nightingale-Conant, and the *Chicken Soup for the Soul* publisher. His 15 books have been published in 18 languages.

As the nation's leading authority on how to eliminate limiting beliefs, Noah delivers private workshops, live events, and online courses that his clients call "MANDATORY for anyone who wants to succeed in life and business."

He also appears frequently in the news worldwide, including ABC, NBC, CBS, Fox, The Hallmark Channel, National Public Radio, *Chicago Sun-Times, Parade, Los Angeles Business Journal, The Washington Post, Woman's Day, Entrepreneur on Fire, Selling Power, Entrepreneur.com, The Jenny McCarthy Show, Costco Connection,* and *The Huffington Post.*

Fun fact: Noah once won an all-expenses-paid trip to Hawaii on the game show *Concentration,* where he missed winning a new car by three seconds. (Note: He had not yet discovered Afformations® or Power Habits®.)

Book Noah to speak at your next event at **BookNoah.com**.